FORGET-ME-NOT LANE

by the same author

A DAY IN THE DEATH OF JOE EGG
THE NATIONAL HEALTH or NURSE NORTON'S AFFAIR

Forget-me-not Lane

Humorous, serious
and dramatic selections
by

PETER NICHOLS

FABER AND FABER
3 Queen Square
London

First published in 1971
by Faber and Faber Limited
3 Queen Square London WC1
Printed in Great Britain by
Latimer Trend & Co Ltd Plymouth
All rights reserved

ISBN 0 571 09855 X (*hard bound edition*)
ISBN 0 571 09857 6 (*paper covered edition*)

822·914
N37

© 1971 by Peter Nichols

THE SONGS
by MARTIN BELL

Continuous, a medley of old pop numbers—
Our lives are like this. Three whistled bars
Are all it takes to catch us, defenceless
On a District Line Platform, sullen to our jobs,
And the thing stays with us all day, still dapper still Astaire,
Still fancy-free. We're dreaming while we work.

Be careful, keep afloat, the past is lapping your chin.
South of the Border is sad boys in khaki
In 1939. And *J'attendrai* a transit camp,
Tents in the dirty sand. Don't go back to Sorrento.
Be brisk and face the day and set your feet
On the sunny side always, the sunny side of the street.

Penguin Modern Poets 3
Reprinted with the permission of the author

My readers . . . Sometimes I imagine them, sullen fleshy inarticulate men, stockbrokers, sellers of goods, living in thirty-year-old detached houses among the golf courses of Outer London, husbands of ageing and bitter wives they first seduced to Artie Shaw's "Begin the Beguine" or The Squadronaires' "The Nearness of You"; fathers of cold-eyed lascivious daughters on the pill, to whom Ramsay Macdonald is coeval with Rameses II, and cannabis-smoking jeans-and-bearded Stuart-haired sons whose oriental contempt for bread is equalled only by their insatiable demand for it; men in whom a pile of scratched coverless 78s in the attic can awaken memories of vomiting blindly from small Tudor windows to Muggsy Spanier's "Sister Kate", or winding up a gramophone in a punt to play Armstrong's "Body and Soul"; men whose first coronary is coming like Christmas; who drift, loaded helplessly with commitments and obligations and necessary observances, into the darkening avenues of age and incapacity, deserted by everything that once made life sweet. These I have tried to remind of the excitement of jazz, and tell where it may still be found.

From the introduction to *All What Jazz* by Philip Larkin (Faber & Faber 1970).

CHARACTERS

Frank, 30–40
Young Frank, 14–21
Ursula, 28–38
Young Urse, 14–19
Charles, 50–75
Amy, 40–65
Ivor, 14–21
Miss 1940, 18+
Mr. Magic, 50

The first performance of *Forget-me-not Lane* was given at the Greenwich Theatre on 1st April 1971, the production subsequently transferring to the Apollo Theatre on 28th April. The cast was as follows:

Frank	ANTON RODGERS
Charles	MICHAEL BATES
Young Frank	IAN GELDER
Amy	JOAN HICKSON
Ivor	MALCOLM McFEE
Mr. Magic	EDDIE MOLLOY
Miss 1940	STEPHANIE LAWRENCE
Ursula	PRISCILLA MORGAN
Young Urse	SANDRA PAYNE

Directed by Michael Blakemore
Designed by Roger Butlin
Costumes by Annena Stubbs
Lighting by Robert Bryan

Semicircular screen contains perhaps six, perhaps eight doors. Closed, they are hardly noticeable.

They open inwards on to the acting area.

With front lights on, the impression is of a plain wall enclosing a space. The space, on the forestage, breaks into a number of levels.

Centre stage is a sofa.

The screen need be no more than ten feet high and the theatre wall can be seen beyond.

One of the doors is open at the beginning and in the opening is a tape-recorder on a cabinet. We are to assume that it's from here that the music comes.

ACT ONE

A record recital for about twenty minutes.
   Opus One *by Tommy Dorsey.*
   That Lovely Week-End *by Vera Lynn.*
   I Wish I Could Shimmy Like My Sister Kate *by Muggsy Spanier.*
   Road to the Isles *by the Red Army Choir.*
   My A.C.W.2 *by The Squadronaires.*
   And the last two:
   Voice of the stars No. 4 (including Will Hay's dialogue about electricity).
   Maple Leaf Rag *by Sidney Bechet.*
   Throughout this, FRANK *comes on and goes off several times. He is forty. First, he brings on a cheap suitcase, open and half-full. He leaves it and goes. On his next appearances, he brings on personal articles and puts them in the case. He pays more attention to the music than the case and often stops to mime to the records, which he knows by heart. At the end of one, he bows to an imaginary audience.*

FRANK (*softly*): Thank you very much. Thank you.
      (*Sometimes he looks into the case and rejects an article.*)
      No, no. . . .
      (*And after returning several times, he says:*)
      What exactly are you doing, man?
      (*He mimes Bechet's soprano sax and turns off the player, takes some small articles from drawers under the player and puts into his pocket (cheque-book, cigarettes, money), brings out handkerchief, holds it up and looks at it, shrugs, returns it to his pocket. Closes the door.*)
      Why don't you leave off packing now?

13

(*Keeps moving.*)

Not as though you show any improvement as a packer. The same feeble indecision . . . same refusal to believe the weather might change . . . shivering through a frost in light-weight suit and pack-a-mac.

(*Now addresses audience directly.*)

And when you consider how large packing has loomed in my family. Both my families. The one I was issued with and the one I escaped to. And eventually from.

(*Takes cigarettes out and lights one. Coughs.*)

Christ.

(*Recovers.*)

When my wife was packing, our bedroom used to look as though we'd had the burglars in. I used to say, "Surely, love, I shan't need six shirts for four days!" I remember that first second honeymoon we went on, I said, "Wellington boots *and* tennis rackets?" And she said, "If you're going to stand there carping, you can do the packing yourself!" "All right," I said, "then let me." "You can't," she said, "you're a hopeless packer." My parents went over the same ground more times than I care to remember. Setting off at last from Bristol to Minehead in the Wolseley, my mother would say, "I hope you packed my laxatives." And Dad: "If your laxatives were listed, they were packed. The old man's not exactly a novice at packing suitcases." Not exactly, no. And yet—in thirty-five years' commercial travelling, he never once got ready on time. Every Monday morning he'd start at dawn with the best intentions but hours later he'd still be ransacking the house for indelible pencils, spectacle cases, samples of cake decorations such as nodding robins on sugar logs . . . or silver horseshoes for wedding-cakes with real bells that tinkled——

(CHARLES *comes on, aged fifty. He wears bowler hat, raincoat, grey spats, blue suit underneath, and carries small leather case.*)

CHARLES: Frank!

FRANK (*remembering*): Hallo?

(*Pause.* CHARLES *takes no notice but looks offstage.*)

CHARLES (*louder*): Frank!

14

YOUNG FRANK (*off*): Hallo?

CHARLES: Hallo who?

YOUNG FRANK (*off*): Hallo, Dad.

CHARLES: Come in here.

FRANK: Trying to get him off was like some primitive attempt at man-powered flight. The great flapping steel wings, the sudden loss of energy——

(YOUNG FRANK *comes on, aged fourteen now and wearing shirt and trousers, carrying newspaper.*)

YOUNG FRANK: What?

CHARLES: What? What's "what"?

YOUNG FRANK: A unit of electricity.

CHARLES: About what are you talking now?

YOUNG FRANK: The schoolmaster sketch. What is a unit of electricity? A watt. That's what I'm asking you. That's what it is.

CHARLES: You great piecan.

(YOUNG FRANK *shrugs, reads.*)

And straighten your shoulders when I'm talking to you, stand up straight.

YOUNG FRANK (*groans*): I'm trying to finish breakfast.

CHARLES: At ten o'clock! Most people have been out, done a day's work by now. Your mother pampers you, gives in to you, she's not got the least idea——

YOUNG FRANK: I'm on holiday. What's the matter with having breakfast——

CHARLES: Wossermarrer? What's wossermarrer?

(YOUNG FRANK *groans, goes on reading.* CHARLES *grabs the lobe of his son's ear and peers into it.*)

Have you washed the wax from your ears?

(YOUNG FRANK *groans, moves away.*)

FRANK: He was like an upset beetle.

CHARLES (*moving about*): I was up this morning at quarter to seven. All this time trying to get away from this house but nobody ever puts anything back where they found it. You been smoking my cigarettes?

YOUNG FRANK: No.

FRANK: But a chill of fear.

15

CHARLES: No who?

YOUNG FRANK: No, Dad.

CHARLES: Well, it's beyond my comprehension. I've never let smoke, strong drink or vile language pass my lips since I signed the pledge at fourteen. Your mother only has the odd cork-tipped.

(*Stands not looking at* YOUNG FRANK *but seems to be expecting a confession. He has the air of a prosecutor with an irrefutable case.*)

YOUNG FRANK: I haven't touched them. Honestly!

(*Pause. Looks at* CHARLES. CHARLES *looks at him.*)

CHARLES (*softer tone*): If you tell me honestly, boy, I believe you.

FRANK: Oh, yes. That sudden Band-of-Hope piety.

(YOUNG FRANK *looks at his paper.*)

Even if I was telling the truth, I'd blush with shame.

CHARLES: And look at me when I'm talking, you great pudden.

(YOUNG FRANK *groans.*)

(AMY *enters from a different door, wearing spring clothes with apron and turban. She is forty.*)

AMY: Here.

(*Gives him two packets of cigarettes.*)

CHARLES: Where were they?

AMY: Pocket of the winter suit you've just left off.

FRANK: She was trying to turn him over and point him in the right direction.

CHARLES (*hopelessly*): Could have sworn I looked in there.

YOUNG FRANK: Told you.

CHARLES: I believed you, Son. I know you're a truthful boy.

FRANK: Still can't tell a lie, even today.

CHARLES: Now that smokes are in short supply, branch managers appreciate a packet on the firm.

AMY: I should think they did——

CHARLES: Mister Steel, the manager of Yeovil branch——

AMY: With queues at every shop.

CHARLES (*after pausing*): Friend Steel of——

AMY: And they say it's going to get worse.

(CHARLES *looks at her.*)

16

CHARLES: Friend Steel of——

AMY: I said: I don't see how it *can* get worse.

CHARLES (*quick and loud*): Friend Steel of Yeovil branch chain-smokes from morn till night and coughs his heart up and turns a lurid purple. I said to him, "Friend, if I speak quite frankly, you're a noodle, coating your lungs with nicotine instead of God's good air."

YOUNG FRANK: Then you passed him another packet?

CHARLES: You've got it, boy, and licked my indelible pencil and said, "Now, Friend, how you off for custard powder? A very good line. Another gross of tins?"

FRANK: Early lessons in commercial duplicity.

AMY: If you don't get a move on he'll be gone to dinner.

CHARLES: Lunch, Amy.

AMY: Lunch, then.

(*He takes off his bowler hat, kisses her, puts it on.*)

CHARLES: See you Friday afternoon.

AMY: Be careful. Got your gas-mask?

CHARLES: In the car.

AMY: And your torch in case there's a power cut?

CHARLES (*looks at list*): Yes. (*To* YOUNG FRANK.) During the air raids, do as your mother tells you.

YOUNG FRANK (*reading paper*): Okay.

CHARLES: Okay? What's okay?

AMY: Don't go on at him.

CHARLES: You spoil him, Amy, you side with him. How long since you had your hair cut? Buzfuz? I'm talking to you.

YOUNG FRANK: Fortnight.

AMY: It does want cutting badly, Frank.

CHARLES: No, Amy, it doesn't want cutting badly, it badly wants cutting. But we want it cut well, not badly.

(*Moves about, staring over audience.*)

FRANK: Of course, he was trying to find a reason not to go.

CHARLES: Just look at the car! Standing there since eight this morning. The only car in the avenue, it looks like showing off. I detest showing off almost as much as I detest foul language or dirty fingernails.

AMY: Now's your chance to move it.

CHARLES: They can't wait to get rid of the old man. Good-bye, Frank.

YOUNG FRANK: 'Bye.

CHARLES: Good-bye who?

(YOUNG FRANK *groans*.)

AMY: Come on.

(*Driven to the door by* AMY, *then turns*.)

CHARLES: I think I'll go down the avenue, save turning the car round, along Appian Terrace and up Tuscan Vale to the main road——

AMY: I should.

(*Pushes him off*.)

(YOUNG FRANK *follows their progress into the wings, downstage and across the front*. FRANK *watches with him*.)

YOUNG FRANK: Go, go, go.

FRANK: Into the lobby where sunlight through Edwardian stained-glass colours the morning's loaf and milk-bottles——

YOUNG FRANK: Don't let him talk any more, Mum——

FRANK: —where open umbrellas stand drying out on rainy days——

YOUNG FRANK: Shut the gate behind him, one last wave——

FRANK: And the only car in the avenue won't be seen again until Friday afternoon.

YOUNG FRANK: Another five days of freedom!

(*First quarter of tinkling Westminster chime as* AMY *comes back carrying loaf and bottles*.)

AMY: Quarter-past ten on washing day. Before I know where I am it's going to be dinner-time and I shan't know where I am. (*Puts down bread and milk. Takes cigarette and matches from apron*.)

YOUNG FRANK: Well, anyway, old Hitler's gone.

AMY: You shouldn't talk like that about your father.

(*Goes to window and looks into street*.)

YOUNG FRANK: He's *worse* than Hitler. Bet you anything Hitler wouldn't stop me using his wind-up gramophone if he already had a great big radiogram!

(*Sees her*.)

What you looking after him for?

18

AMY: Make sure he's gone.

YOUNG FRANK: He knows you smoke.

AMY: He doesn't like it.

(*Comes down and lights up.*)

YOUNG FRANK: He doesn't like anything. Smoking, drinking, being with your friends and wearing the kind of clothes you——

AMY: He's got his funny ways.

YOUNG FRANK: He's a cruel tyrant.

(*He pronounces it tirrant.*)

AMY: Cruel what?

YOUNG FRANK: Tyrant! This is a tyranny. He tries to crush the spirit of freedom.

FRANK: I can't have said that. Tirrant?

AMY: He's done his best for you, Frank. Put you through a good school——

YOUNG FRANK (*incredulous*): Good school?

FRANK: With a Latin song and motto.

YOUNG FRANK (*to him*): But no girls.

AMY: Saved up all that money in cerstificates that you can draw when you're twenty-one.

YOUNG FRANK (*correcting*): Certificates.

AMY: Yes. Cerstificates.

YOUNG FRANK: I don't want money. I want liberty. I think everyone should be allowed to do as they like all the time.

AMY: Don't talk silly.

YOUNG FRANK: I think everyone should be happy and go out in the fields and have picnics and—you know—take all their clothes off even, if they want to——

AMY: That *would* look nice, I must say.

YOUNG FRANK: —and sing and dance and just be friends and no one would have too much to eat while other people haven't got enough——

FRANK: Oh, no!

(*Embarrassed, he hides his face with his hand.*)

YOUNG FRANK: —and people would stop hating each other.

FRANK: It sounds like a Pop Festival.

AMY: Have you finished your breakfast?

YOUNG FRANK: Can't you see, Mum, that it's wrong for people to fight each other when they could be loving each other?

AMY: Aren't we supposed to fight the Germans then?

YOUNG FRANK: If we'd never started, they couldn't have had a war. But now, yes, I suppose we've got to have soldiers and all——

AMY: And aren't the soldiers coming on the picnics?

YOUNG FRANK: They can't, can they, till the war's over. Then everyone has got to be friends and go out into the fields together, sharing and loving——

AMY: And what about the poor people from Mina Road? The dirty boys from the elementary schools. I can't somehow see you enjoying a picnic with them. Spitting and using nasty language.

YOUNG FRANK: You're talking as though it's all going to happen *now*, with everybody just as they *are* now. But all the people who don't agree with freedom will be put in special places to be educated. And if they still don't want to be free, they'll be put on desert islands. People like Goering and Mussolini and Dad.

AMY: I see, as the blind man said.

(*Suddenly worried.*)

If everyone's just enjoying themselves, who's going to clear up all the mess?

YOUNG FRANK: Mess?

AMY: After the picnics.

YOUNG FRANK: Machines. Some huge great vacuum cleaner. Machines will do all the work.

AMY: That'll be nice. Meantime I'd better get the copper going. Or before I know where I am, it'll be dinner-time and I shan't know where I am.

(*She makes to leave.* YOUNG FRANK *reads paper.*)

FRANK: I know!

(*Air-raid siren sounds the alert.*)

AMY: Oh, not those devils again!

(*Goes to window to look out.*)

YOUNG FRANK: Mum! You say I shouldn't call him Hitler but think how he stopped you singing.

AMY (*turning back*): I had a lovely singing voice. Mister Dunn
the adjudicator said I was a natural soprano with perfect
pitch and a wide range and all I needed was experience.

FRANK: The self-pity!

YOUNG FRANK: But he was jealous. He wouldn't let you follow
your career because it would have meant you singing for
other people, not just him.

AMY: I couldn't follow a career with you on the way.

YOUNG FRANK: Well after! You could have taken it up again after.
I could have come on tour with you in the opera company.

AMY (*drawing on cigarette and blowing out smoke*): It wouldn't
have been fair on him. Or you. He doesn't even like me
doing these shows for the troops.

(*Gunfire. They take no notice.*)

He is a miserable devil in some ways. I sometimes wish I'd
never bumped into him at that dance. He was acting the
goat and like a fool I laughed. Well, before I knew it we
were out there doing the fox-trot and the whole floor
stopped to watch us. He was like a gazelle in those days
with his patent pumps and his hair smarmed down.

FRANK: Like *Carnet de Bal*? Remember that film?

(AMY *blows nose with handkerchief. Makes for door.* YOUNG
FRANK *returns to paper.*)

AMY: Did you wet the bed last night?

YOUNG FRANK: Yep.

FRANK: As usual.

AMY: Do try not to.

YOUNG FRANK: I *do*.

AMY: I know you do. Well, get your pyjamas and sheets and
if the one on top's not too damp, only bring the bottom
one and get a clean——

YOUNG FRANK: All right. Later on.

(*Loud gunfire.*)

AMY: Poor Mother, all alone! She hates the gunfire. Twice in
my lifetime those German devils have started a war with
us. When my brothers came home from the trenches,
Mother made them take off their uniforms in the yard, they
were so infested with lice.

YOUNG FRANK: She ought to come and live here.

AMY: She and Dad are at each other's throats, she says she'd rather be independent.

FRANK: He couldn't stand the sight of Grandma drinking stout.
(*Front door slams off.*)

AMY: What's that?
(*Looks out of window.*)
Oh, no, the car's outside.
(CHARLES *enters, as before, but carrying one shoe in front of him, at arm's length.*)

YOUNG FRANK: What you doing back?

CHARLES: Mister Dick was filling Leonora with petrol when the sirens went. I said, "There's not the slightest use rushing off to Yeovil now. Friend Steel makes straight for the convenience the moment a raid begins and for some time afterwards he's quite unable to bring his mind to bear on cake decorations and desiccated coconut."

AMY: What you holding out your shoe for?

CHARLES: D'you want to hear my story or not?

YOUNG FRANK: Not much.

CHARLES: Hold your tongue, Buzfuz. I'm talking to Woodbine Winnie here. "In fact," I added, "I think there's very little point in leaving now till after lunch."
(YOUNG FRANK *and* AMY *groan. Gunfire.*)

AMY: The larder's empty.

CHARLES: And Mister Dick said, "They won't cheer to see you back." I said, "I don't care tuppence."

AMY: But what's the shoe for?

CHARLES: Crossing the pavement from the car, I'm dashed if I didn't inadvertently step where a dog had used the convenience!

AMY: Fancy bringing it in the dining-room!

CHARLES: I'm on my way to wipe it clean with a copy of *Reynolds News*. But it's beyond my comprehension—after I'd put up a notice: Dogs not to foul the public footway.

YOUNG FRANK: Lot of dogs round here can't read.

CHARLES: Don't try to score off me, Sonny Jim. You're not half bright enough!

(Moves towards other door.)

And you can help me open the garage doors, we'll put the car away, it might get struck by shrapnel out there.

(Goes. AMY *has picked up bread and milk.)*

AMY: Don't make a mess in my clean scullery.

(Goes after him. YOUNG FRANK *appeals to ceiling.)*

YOUNG FRANK: Oh, God, please help us to be free of him. Please make a bomb fall on him, God.

(Goes off other way with newspaper.)

FRANK: How could I possibly understand them at fourteen? Their complicated middle-aged game of regret and recrimination? My own experience was confined to chasing high-school girls through the city museum at lunch-time. Oh, those stuffed kangaroos! Those tableaux of British wild-life! That scent of gravy! I took a party of students last week and I'm glad to say it's resisted all attempts at modernization. The hippopotamus still yawns beside the fire buckets.

(Screws his eyes tight shut and claps his hands.)

Stick to the point, man! The point was that I couldn't understand the sophisticated war my parents were con-ducting—either the issues or the strategy. But I *was* in the line of fire. So instead of understanding I took sides. Dad was a monster, Mum a martyr. But it might have been just as true the other way: Mum a shrew, and Dad henpecked. What did my own boy make of it when at thirteen he watched Ursula and me growling and roaring at each other? Yes, that's one of the reasons I left her. Having seen my parents like cat-and-dog year after year, I wanted to save my son that spectacle.

(Ponders. To himself.)

But is it too late to start again?

(Shrugs.)

Sometimes wish I *had* been evacuated to North America. It was soon after the air-raids started. Had my shrapnel collection all ready. Used to dream of Canadian girls with dancing eyes all mad to kiss the brave British boy who was so modest about the bombs. The boy who had miraculously

23

stopped wetting the bed. But then a liner was sunk in mid-Atlantic and children drowned so the scheme was called off. I'm not sorry *really*. What Did You Do In The War, Daddy? Played ice-hockey in Montreal? In any case, the war only seemed a caricature of family life. (*Churchill imitation.*) We shall fight on the landing-grounds, we shall fight in the living-rooms, we shall fight in the only car in the avenue. . . . Everyone was exhorted to take sides at the time and Dad became my personal Hitler, just as *he* rejected *his*, a drunken butcher, and clung to his forbidding mother. She got him to sing songs against Demon Drink in the temperance society and his dad caught him coming out and cuffed him across the ear, which made him slightly deaf from that day on.

(*One of the doors opens and* CHARLES *looks out.*)

CHARLES: I heard that.

FRANK: You always heard what you wanted to.

CHARLES (*coming on*): Mother was a wonderful woman.

FRANK: I didn't say she wasn't.

CHARLES: You used the word "forbidding".

FRANK: She was trying to drag her family up the first rungs of the social ladder out of pubs and music-halls into a street with small front gardens.

CHARLES: Of course she was.

FRANK: Yes, right. Social mobility.

CHARLES: You blaming her for that?

FRANK: No.

CHARLES: You might not be a lecturer in Sociology if she hadn't made us pull ourselves up by our boot-straps.

FRANK: Agreed.

CHARLES (*to audience*): Lecturer at a Technical College, this great coon. Never believe it, would you?

(FRANK *shrugs to audience.*)

Stand up straight, hold your shoulders back.

FRANK: When I said "forbidding" I meant she was against pleasure. Perhaps she had to be.

CHARLES: Pleasure? I was there, boy, I saw the Good Olde Days at first hand. Ours was the only family whose blankets didn't go to Ikey Stein the pawnbroker every Monday morn-

24

ing to be reclaimed every Friday night! No thanks to the old man who no sooner got a few bob in his pocket than he was round at the four-ale bar.

(*Caricature of drunk.*)

"'Gish another pint, friend, and—hic!—have one yourself."

FRANK: He sounds generous at any rate.

CHARLES: With his cronies, yes, at the bookmaker's or the public-house. But in the bosom of the family, boy, he threw money about like a Jew with no arms.

FRANK: Perhaps it's something he was driven to.

CHARLES: Driven to? What's "driven to"? He was driven to it as pointlessly as you seem to be driven to end sentences with prepositions.

FRANK: Obsolete! That's one of the set of obsolete taboos you expected me to face my twentieth-century adolescence with.

CHARLES: With which you expected me to face my——

FRANK: No wonder I wet the bed three times a week at fourteen!

CHARLES: Don't talk big, you make yourself look small.

FRANK: Get out!

(FRANK *rushes at him,* CHARLES *retreats through door and* FRANK *slams it and returns to centre. Door reopens.*)

CHARLES (*looking out*): You great pudden!

(*Goes, shutting door.*)

(FRANK *looks at door, then again at audience.*)

FRANK: Drink, strong language, the race-track, infidelity and never end a sentence with a preposition. Along with a deep respect for your mother. A decent programme but it wasn't decency I was after. I longed to be delivered into temptation but the nearest I ever came to forbidden fruit was an occasional Carmen Miranda film.

(*Glances at the door* CHARLES *came from. Goes on quietly.*)

Poor man. Thirty years too late I can see what he must have been suffering, separated from his beloved wife five days a week, packed off gladly Monday mornings to share commercial hotels with heavy-drinking, dirty-joke-telling travellers. And on Friday welcomed back as warmly as a Messerschmitt.

(YOUNG FRANK *comes on, opens door to gramophone. Puts*

record on. Scratched 1941 "Woodchoppers' Ball" by Joe
Loss (or Woody Herman).)

(YOUNG FRANK *is wearing a suit and polished shoes. He*
conducts the band, mimes tenor sax.)

Especially by me and my close friend Ivor.

(IVOR *comes on from the same door that* FRANK *used,*
arriving just in time to mime the clarinet solo. YOUNG FRANK
signals him in and keeps the band quieter so he can be heard.
IVOR *is fourteen as well and also wears a suit.)*

(*After listening for a while*): This was just before we moved
from swing to jazz.

(CHARLES *enters from another door, behind the boys. He is*
dressed as before but carries a case in one hand, a bunch of
flowers in the other. He puts down case, frowns at oblivious
boys and takes off the record. YOUNG FRANK *and* IVOR *see*
him and groan.)

CHARLES: I can hear that blessed racket on the far side of the
street.

YOUNG FRANK: You home again?

CHARLES: The usual sunny welcome.

(YOUNG FRANK *makes face at* IVOR. IVOR *facially imitates*
CHARLES. CHARLES *looks closely at record-player.)*

And still using steel needles, tearing your records to shreds.
Why don't you take a bone one?

YOUNG FRANK: 'Cause they sound terrible. You can hardly——

CHARLES: Hullo, Ivor, are you quite well?

IVOR: Hullo.

CHARLES: Hullo who?

IVOR: Hullo, Mister Bisley, I suppose.

CHARLES: And stand up straight when you speak to me. Stoop-
ing over like that, how can you expect to fill your lungs
with God's good air?

IVOR (*giggles*): Good old God.

CHARLES: What d'you say?

(*But a piano is played offstage. Sinding's "Rustle of*
Spring".) Listen to that—your mother playing. Always been
one of my greatest pleasures, Frank, hearing your mother
play.

26

YOUNG FRANK: As a matter of fact——

CHARLES: Hold your tongue, boy, give yourself a chance to hear some decent music for a change. I shall go to her, throw open the door, and drop on one knee before her, saying, "You, my dear, are playing *Rustle of Spring* and I've brought you a spring bouquet." What do you think she'll say to that, boy? "You home again?"

YOUNG FRANK: No, she'll probably say, "That's not me playing, it's my pupil." She's giving a lesson.

(*A mistake in the music, which has otherwise been adequate. Pause. The pianist begins again from a few bars back.*)

CHARLES (*without conviction*): Fancy playing records when your mother's teaching!

(*Puts flowers on table.* IVOR *moves to* YOUNG FRANK *and whispers.*)

YOUNG FRANK: Going up the back room.

CHARLES: Why are you both in your best?

IVOR: We're entertaining tonight.

YOUNG FRANK: An anti-aircraft station.

FRANK: Or fighter base or military hospital or isolated wireless unit.

CHARLES: Your mother, too?

YOUNG FRANK: We're all in the same concert-party, you know that.

(CHARLES *glares, betrayed, towards the piano music.*)

CHARLES: And I've been away since Monday! She promised she wouldn't go entertaining Friday night.

YOUNG FRANK: We've got to pull our weight.

FRANK (*to* YOUNG FRANK): Show a bit of understanding.

IVOR: If the troops want us, we've got to go.

CHARLES: What makes you think they want you?

(*Imitates Sergeant.*)

"Fifty volunteers to watch some crackpots do a concert, the others will peel the spuds." That's how it's done.

YOUNG FRANK: How d'you know? You've never been in the army. Dodged both wars.

CHARLES: I was medically unfit in the first due to the deafness caused by my father clouting me across the ear.

27

YOUNG FRANK: Any case, our show's much better than you and your corny old recitations.

CHARLES (*quietly*): Not so much of the jolly old buck. You don't know about what you're talking. Haven't you ever read my notices? Ivor, you?

IVOR: Yeah.

CHARLES: "If laughing ensures growing fat, each of the audience must bulk considerably as a result of Charles Bisley's sketches of London low-life." "One cannot too highly praise Mr. Bisley's characterization of Ikey Cohen." But there was the unfortunate occasion when I deputized for another entertainer at a function and thought I'd kick off with one of my most popular songs *Sergeant Solomon Isaac Stein.* I was only half-way through when they started throwing pennies, boy. I finished and got off quick. When the lights went on, I looked at the audience. By Jove, you could have hung a bunch of keys on every nose. It was a Jewish dinner.

(*Roars with laughter. They watch impassively.*)

I was never invited back.

IVOR: Well, anyway, I reckon we all ought to do our bit.

YOUNG FRANK: Remember what old Winnie said: "I have nothing to offer but blood, toil, tears and sweat."

CHARLES: Acting the goat in a concert-party is not exactly what Mister Churchill strove to convey by those beautiful words.

(*They groan.* IVOR *imitates* CHARLES *facially.*)

It's a pity you don't put some of your blood, toil, tears and sweat into your school work. Pass your exams and get a job in the Civil Service.

FRANK: Which is what I did in the end. Some years later.

CHARLES: Have you done your prep for tomorrow?

YOUNG FRANK: I can do it in the break.

CHARLES: You sprawl about in your best clothes, listening to rubbish and tell me you can do your prep in the break?

YOUNG FRANK: It's only revision and I'm nearly top in French, anyway.

CHARLES: *Nearly* top's not good enough. One day, when the

war's over and France is liberated, you may go as your mother and I did and how glad I was to know a little of the language. No one could claim your mother had the gift of tongues and like a piecan she said to a lady in the hotel: "Can you tell us the way to Marshal Joffre street?" I said, "Amy, for goodness' sake, stand aside, let the old man. Ou est le Rue de Marshal Joffre, s'il vous plait, Madame?" She said as quick as a flash, "A le droit, Monsieur, a le droit."

(*They wince at his accent.*)

IVOR: Lucky she was a Cockney, too.

(YOUNG FRANK *laughs.*)

CHARLES: You give me cheek in my house, you won't come here again, Sonny Jim.

FRANK: The strongest threat he could use. Ivor was my life.

YOUNG FRANK: I've only got to revise the subjunctive of irregular verbs from *devoir* to *ouvrir* and I know them all already, Dad. Honestly.

CHARLES (*quietly*): You tell me honestly, boy, I believe you.

(YOUNG FRANK *looks at floor. The rustle of spring has passed by and the pupil is playing scales.* CHARLES *looks towards the sound then back again.*)

Right, Ivor, in this bag are one or two presents from branch managers.

FRANK: The few he hadn't estranged by his Puritanism.

CHARLES: A pound of bacon from Wiltshire, a Battenburg cake from Cardiff and a tin of salmon from Glastonbury.

IVOR: Black market.

CHARLES: Not at all. I'm in the distributive trades and fragments are bound to fall off here and there in the process of conveying the goods from hither to yon.

IVOR: Okay.

CHARLES: I haven't noticed your father averse to the odd hand-out.

FRANK: All the same it was wicked at a time when most people welcomed rationing as a first step towards some degree of fair shares.

CHARLES: Come here, Son.

FRANK: A step not even the ruling class could postpone any
longer.

(CHARLES *gives* IVOR *the case*.)

CHARLES: Take it to the scullery and as you pass through the
music-room——

YOUNG FRANK: The music-room?

CHARLES: Hold your tongue! As you pass through, look un-
concerned, don't draw the pupil's attention to the suitcase
in any way.

IVOR: She's only eleven.

CHARLES: If you paid more attention to what's going on in the
world, you'd know children have been betraying their own
parents in Germany.

FRANK: We had this pantomime every Friday because he was
really excited by the thought of wickedness.

CHARLES: And take these flowers——

FRANK: Afraid of every kind of pleasure he had put behind him
when he rose from the Edwardian poor.

CHARLES: Fill with water the vawse, vayse or vahse you will find
on the window-sill and place them therein. Who said that,
the old man? I'll give him a kick in the pants.

(*Kicks himself, laughs*.)

IVOR: Okay.

(*Takes case and flowers and goes*.)

CHARLES: Got one or two more cases you can help bring in
from the car, Frank. The longer I leave it standing there,
the more it looks like showing off.

(YOUNG FRANK *goes and* CHARLES *follows. Piano practice
finishes*.)

FRANK: Having stowed the plunder, my mother and Ivor and I
would catch the bus to meet the cars that took us into the
country where we did Our Bit. And when I say Our Bit, I
should explain for the benefit of anybody taking hash and
wearing old curtains and their mum's beads that I don't
mean doing our thing or our bag. . . . No, doing our
bit meant helping to win the war. And grotesque as it may
seem now, we believed it. Sometimes we'd have to shout
through gunfire and . . . once I remember at a fighter station,

the audience were called into the air one by one and those
that stayed shouted, "Carry on!" Perhaps Dad was right
and it was a choice between watching us and cookhouse
fatigues. But we never believed it. . . .

(*Union Jack unfurls at back. Concert party piano plays
elaborate introduction.* AMY *enters in velvet evening gown
with pearl necklace.*)

AMY (*sings*):

> THERE'LL ALWAYS BE AN ENGLAND
> WHILE THERE'S A COUNTRY LANE,
> WHEREVER THERE'S A COTTAGE SMALL
> BESIDE A FIELD OF GRAIN.

(*A middle-aged man enters in the costume and make-up of a
Chinese magician. While* AMY *continues, he shows a number
of separate silk squares: red, white and blue.* YOUNG FRANK
comes on with a Chinese kimono and shows an empty cylinder,
MISTER MAGIC *puts the squares into the cylinder.*)

> THERE'LL ALWAYS BE AN ENGLAND
> WHERE THERE'S A CROWDED STREET
> WHEREVER THERE'S A CHIMNEY TALL,
> A MILLION MARCHING FEET.

(IVOR, *as before, comes on and opens a door behind which is
a large sketch-pad. He begins a drawing while* MISTER MAGIC
and FRANK *continue packing squares into cylinder.*)

> RED, WHITE AND BLUE
> WHAT DOES IT MEAN TO YOU?
> SURELY YOU'RE PROUD,
> SHOUT IT ALOUD,
> BRITONS, AWAKE!

(*A* YOUNG BLONDE *wearing Union Jack satin briefs roller-
skates on and begins tap-dancing.*)

> THE EMPIRE TOO,
> WE CAN DEPEND ON YOU
> FREEDOM REMAINS
> THESE ARE THE CHAINS
> NOTHING CAN BREAK.

CHORUS:

> THERE'LL ALWAYS BE AN ENGLAND.

31

(FRANK *holds cylinder and* MISTER MAGIC *takes from it the first square, now a Union Jack. He walks across the stage and pulls out a long tape strung with flags.*)

AND ENGLAND SHALL BE FREE——

(*They point to* IVOR'*s drawing, which is now seen to be a caricature of Churchill.*)

IF ENGLAND MEANS AS MUCH TO YOU——

(*They form a line downstage and the* DANCER *finishes by doing the splits, her hands held by* FRANK *and* IVOR.)

AS ENGLAND MEANS TO ME.

(*Coda and Arpeggios from pianist. They all wave and bow. Then go. Flag fades, door shut.*)

FRANK: We never gave a thought to the old man at home, listening to Beethoven, sharpening his bone needles, imagining our wickedness. He had a lively, Puritanical imagination. His pleasure came from resisting and thinking the world far naughtier than it was. Pubs he had always pictured to me as Dickensian dens where men and women assaulted each other while their children waited in the dark outside. About this time we rehearsed our show in the upstairs room of a city pub, among the emblems of the Order of Buffaloes, so I was at last allowed to glimpse these horrors for myself. And surprise, they seemed to be drab parlours full of old-age pensioners. So God knows what he thought we were doing on our evenings out! I wasn't bothered either. My only thought was for the peroxide blonde.

(MISS 1940 *re-enters without skates.*)

At eighteen, only four years older, she was already a different generation. Soldiers roared at her satin drawers, her legs browned with liquid make-up. I roared too but silently, inside my head. "Please, God, let her sit beside me in the car home." Not that I ever *did* anything . . . but I could smell the powder, feel the warmth, the beat of her heart, the rise and fall of her breasts. . . . One night she sat on my hand. (*She sits on his hand on the sofa.*) I couldn't think how to tell her. An hour the journey took and when we dropped her, my fingers were paralysed. Nobody noticed. Nobody ever noticed us much. It was a time for grown-up people. And a

32

we approached the city, the sky was orange, searchlight
beams were trying to find the bombers, a balloon burned
over the houses, the ack-ack pounded away. . . . And my
hand was crushed beneath a dancer's thighs!
(*Exit* MISS 1940.)

Next day I was expected to be fourteen again and decline
irregular verbs . . . from *devoir* to *ouvrir* . . . but all we wanted,
the back row boys, throughout Divinity and Elementary
Science, was the air-raid alert and orderly evacuation
following coloured arrows to the nearest shelter. Divinity
was best because from this room we scuttled to the base-
ment laboratories of the nearby university. And here we
gathered with our grubby minds to snigger at glass jars
full of pickled human embryos . . . while the more clean-
living boys identified the sounds of enemy aircraft. (*Moves
excitedly.*) Then down to the City Museum at lunch-time.
British Wildlife had been hit by incendiaries but we chased
the high-school girls through Transport Down The Ages
and struggled with them behind the horse-drawn fire-engines.
(URSULA *comes on, aged 38, attractive and well-dressed.*)
(*To her.*) You were about thirteen.

URSULA: Thinking about me again. You said you wouldn't.

FRANK: I find those years exciting to remember.

URSULA: I expect the peroxide blonde does too.

FRANK: She must be among those middle-aged women who flock
the local palais on Glenn Miller night. But at least she'll
have some memories worth having. Whereas mine! God!

URSULA: Whose fault's that?

FRANK: Mine, I know.

URSULA: I tried hard enough. From the first moment I saw you.

FRANK: You didn't make it very obvious.

URSULA: You were too busy being scathing and sophisticated to
notice.

FRANK: Pride.

URSULA: Yes. But a deep disapproval of pleasure, too. An urge
to spoil people's fun.

FRANK: Only because I was afraid.

URSULA: No. You're still like that. Have you had any girls since

you left me? No. You spend most of your spare time
dwelling on your lost opportunities. Remembering the war.

FRANK: Pleasure's only part of life. When we lived together, I
used to say I had two interests. One: to be of use to my
fellow-men. And two: to arouse your slumbering sexuality.

URSULA: You never failed, my love.

(*They are standing some distance from each other.*)

FRANK: Well, the war was the last time, it seems to me, that
pleasure and duty coincided. When they weren't chasing
U-boats and incendiary bombs, the men and women of that
time seemed to be chasing each other.

URSULA: Especially after the Yanks arrived.

FRANK: Yes, skidding about the semis in their sexy jeeps with
tight-arsed trousers and Hollywood names. And the good-
times girls used to——

URSULA: Good-times girls!

(*She laughs.*)

FRANK: They used to sit in rows on our front wall waiting for
their lovers to pour from the evacuated orphanage. My
grandma called them brazen hussies. To me, they were at
least as astonishing as the camel that came by once with a
circus and started nibbling our privet.

URSULA: Ours was a more dismal sector. Pig farms and railways
and a Yankee maintenance unit. The fields and gardens
reeked of oil and boiling pig-food.

FRANK: Ivor and I used to pass through sometimes. Following
the G.I.'s with their tarts up on to the Downs between the
mental homes and the radar installations.

URSULA: I was arrested for loitering once.

FRANK: Did you really pick up Yanks?

URSULA: No. Mum lost her temper and told the policeman I was
only fourteen and still at school but that meant nothing.

FRANK: Most of the tarts weren't that much older.

URSULA: Exactly. My uncle, standing in for Dad till he came
home from the army, threatened me with the strap if I so
much as spoke to them.

FRANK: I suppose I went with them more than she did.

URSULA: What?

FRANK: No. Nothing.

URSULA: The nearest I got was spending so much time with Denise Carter.

(*During her reminiscence,* FRANK *pours a bottle of beer into a glass. Sips it, seeming not to listen to her.*)

Her husband was a garage mechanic, never seen out of oily dungarees. She was very small, Denise, I suppose she'd have said "petite", and as with all these nympho types, scrupulous about the house. The first thing every day was to clean it from top to bottom. She never seemed to entertain the idea of excitement till she'd done that. Then she'd go to her bedroom and during school holidays I'd be allowed to smoke a Lucky Strike with her. I suppose she must have been flat-chested and putty-coloured but by the time she'd got on her painted face with the huge crimson lips and plucked and pencilled her eyebrows and vaselined her lashes . . . curled her hair with sugar and water . . . pushed her breasts up into the padded brassière . . . and climbed into a low-neck magenta sweater in brushed angora, she seemed to me like a film-star. And when you consider some of the oddities we tried to look like then——

FRANK (*nodding*): She probably did, yes.

URSULA: Then Mrs. Lawrence, her friend, would come in, dressed up too, but not so much. She and Denise appeared to be close but I felt she was scandalized and enjoyed carrying gossip to the more respectable women.

FRANK: Can't have been many of *them* left.

URSULA: No. Well, soon after, the pair of them would parade up the street. You should have seen that walk.

FRANK: Were platform soles then or later?

URSULA: While the Americans were here, she promoted herself through the ranks from Private to Major. The Major used to sit smiling, saying, "But, Baby, I'm a married man." And Denise would go and sit on his lap and kiss him, kicking up one leg, the way she'd seen them in the films.

FRANK: Did you ever see any more?

URSULA: They always packed me off before the real business started——

FRANK: If there was any.

URSULA: May not have been. Her husband would have killed her, if he'd found anything. Sometimes there were soldiers when he got home, playing the radiogram and he'd say, "Looks like a party," and wash the oil from his hands, the only concession he made to social life, he always kept on his dungarees. Sometimes he'd get out the projector and show Mickey Mouse films or Popeye. Mrs. Lawrence used to be Olive Oil because her name was Olive and Denise used to be Betty Boop. The Major brought them Betty Boop and Olive Oil badges. And there we'd sit in this weird room, like a half-finished furniture display, drinking beer and nibbling candy, watching these cartoons.

(FRANK *has been smiling appreciatively.*)

FRANK: Hands across the sea.

URSULA: Yes.

FRANK (*Churchill*): Give us the tools and we will finish the job. (*She laughs.*)
   While you were being initiated in the ways of women, Ivor and I were playing puberty games in the back room.

URSULA: That back room!

(IVOR *enters, opening screen of pin-up pictures up to 1943.*)

FRANK: You didn't come there till you were fourteen.

URSULA: Will there ever be a sexier room?

FRANK: One afternoon, if you'd been five minutes earlier, you'd have caught us at our games.

(IVOR, *now sixteen and in sports clothes, takes cigarette from tin and lights up.*)

URSULA: What games?

FRANK: I suppose there's no harm telling you now.

URSULA: What harm could there be?

FRANK: Losing face.

URSULA: What does it matter now?

FRANK: I might want to come back to you.

URSULA: What you did at sixteen couldn't count one way or another, I shan't have you back, I've told you.

FRANK: All right.

(YOUNG FRANK *follows* IVOR. *Now sixteen, wears Mother's*

36

headscarf, skirt, shoes, blouse, padded brassière; also lipstick, pencilled eyebrows, rouged cheeks, etc.)

URSULA: Oh, no!

FRANK: Yes.

YOUNG FRANK: Give us a cigarette.

(IVOR *offers tin.* YOUNG FRANK *lights up.*)

URSULA (*laughing*): Why didn't you ever tell me?

(FRANK *shrugs, watching her watch* YOUNG FRANK.)

And now you sit here wishing you had. Wondering what I'd have said.

FRANK: Yes.

URSULA: It's Denise Carter to the life!

IVOR: That was terrific, man!

(YOUNG FRANK *opens a door and takes out his clothes.*)

YOUNG FRANK: Yeah.

IVOR: What about when old—what's her name—The Burglar? What's her real name?

YOUNG FRANK: Mrs. Parr.

IVOR: Yeah, what about when she said, "Hullo, Ivor," to me and just looked down her nose at you as though you were a Yankee's tart.

YOUNG FRANK: But what about the Yank sentry? (*He takes off make-up.*) What did you do when he whistled after me?

IVOR: Nothing.

YOUNG FRANK: I felt all funny. Bit scared.

URSULA (*sympathetically*): Aaah! (*Goes to* FRANK *and kisses him, maternally.*)

IVOR: Hey, be great if your mum wears these clothes next time she goes past the orphanage and that Yank whistles at her thinking it's you again.

YOUNG FRANK: They whistle at Amy anyway.

IVOR: My old man said, "Those Yanks go for anything in skirts between eight and eighty."

YOUNG FRANK: Old Philip would say that, wallowing about and dreaming of terrific sexual orgies. (*Hard "g".*) The English are all jealous, cause the Yanks get all the girls . . . but I'd go with a Yank if I was a girl.

URSULA: Does that mean, if Ivor hadn't been with you, you'd have spoken to the sentry?

FRANK: I'd never even have gone outside alone. Now I think of it, people must have known I was a boy. They *must* have.

IVOR: Hey, man, you know when you toss off——

YOUNG FRANK: Yeah.

IVOR: —d'you pretend you're a man or a woman?

YOUNG FRANK: I keep changing about. Sometimes I'm a slave girl like Hedy Lamarr and my master whips me a lot and I cringe and beg for mercy. Then I come in as the brave bloke——

IVOR: Alan Ladd?

YOUNG FRANK: Yeah. And beat up this cruel bloke and then I'm Hedy Lamarr again and terrifically glad I shan't be whipped any more . . . so I take me in my arms and surrender . . . then I'm the brave bloke and hold her tight . . . keep changing round.

IVOR: I pretend I'm the bloke all the time.

(*They smoke for a while.* IVOR *coughs.* YOUNG FRANK *begins changing into his own clothes.*)

YOUNG FRANK: Hey, you know Jacobs in Four A.

IVOR: Terrific swot, yeah.

YOUNG FRANK: I saw his tool when we changed for gym. You seen it?

IVOR: No.

YOUNG FRANK: It's different to everyone else's.

IVOR: More like a knob?

YOUNG FRANK: Yeah.

IVOR: I've seen some like that.

FRANK: We knew so little about the Jews.

URSULA: They were in the Bible and Shakespeare.

FRANK: But that was nothing to do with Jacobs of Four A.

URSULA: And my uncle sometimes made a veiled remark about band-leaders.

FRANK: There was Dad's Ikey Cohen . . . but when you think what was happening a few hundred miles away!

URSULA: And our history lessons were still about Clive and Wolfe and Arkwright's Spinning Jenny.

YOUNG FRANK: Another thing about old Jacobs—he never does Divinity.

IVOR: Wish I didn't. Divinity's a dead loss.

YOUNG FRANK: Only thing, you'd miss seeing the unborn babies when the sirens go.

IVOR: Old Muller doesn't do Divinity.

YOUNG FRANK: Muller's an atheist.

IVOR: So am I an atheist.

YOUNG FRANK: But you're not *down* as an atheist. Your old man's got to put you *down*.

IVOR: Fat chance with mine.

YOUNG FRANK: Or mine. (*Imitates Charles.*) "Don't take the Lord's name in vain, boy."

IVOR (*also imitates*): "Get out in God's good air, you great coon."

URSULA: Your poor father. What chance did he have?

FRANK: No more than I had with mine.

YOUNG FRANK: Know what old Muller told me?

IVOR: What?

YOUNG FRANK: If a bod and a woman are shagging and she gets frightened by a mouse or something, her minge can tighten up and the bod can't get it out.

IVOR: Togger White told me that. He said they come from the hospital and throw buckets of water over them and——

YOUNG FRANK: Cri-kee!

IVOR: —if that doesn't loosen it, they have to put them on a stretcher and carry them out to the ambulance.

YOUNG FRANK: With all the neighbours looking!

IVOR: And sometimes they have to operate.

YOUNG FRANK: Cut it off?

IVOR: He didn't say. He said it used to happen a lot during the Blitz. A bomb used to frighten the woman and—— (*Makes strangled face and sounds.*)

YOUNG FRANK: Terrific agony, man.

IVOR: Terrific embarrassment. Would you like to have been a woman?

YOUNG FRANK: No.

IVOR: Wish you had been. Be wizard to be terrific friends with a woman.

YOUNG FRANK: Wouldn't have minded having tits.

(*Now he has changed into boy's shoes, trousers, etc., but still wears bra. Pushes out his chest.* IVOR *touches the padded bra.*)

FRANK: That's enough!

(*Doorbell rings. They jump up.*)

IVOR: Your mum?

YOUNG FRANK: She's at the aircraft factory. And Hitler's in Newton Abbot till Friday. You go and see.

(YOUNG FRANK *fans away smoke, puts on record of Chicago jazz.* IVOR *goes.*)

URSULA: I always passed your house on the way home and when I saw Ivor's bike outside I knew you must be in. Of course it was safe if there were two of you.

FRANK: You'd have been even safer alone. I used to kiss you sometimes in front of Ivor just to prove myself.

URSULA: But I didn't know that. I thought you were experienced.

FRANK: The lost opportunities!

(YOUNG FRANK *has finished change. Puts away Mother's clothes.* IVOR *returns with* YOUNG URSE, *fourteen and wearing school uniform and carrying satchel.* YOUNG FRANK *is jazzing. He sees her and groans.*)

YOUNG URSE: Terrific pong.

YOUNG FRANK: We been smoking.

YOUNG URSE: Pong of lipstick.

(*Pause.*)

IVOR: Been making up. We're going to do a Marx Brothers sketch at the end-of-term show.

YOUNG URSE (*approaching* YOUNG FRANK): Still got some on your face. Smells nice. Sexy.

(*She touches his face, smells her hand.* IVOR *and* YOUNG FRANK *groan.* IVOR *lies on divan.* YOUNG URSE *goes to look at pin-ups.*)

This Harry James?

(*Boys croak and groan with laughter.*)

YOUNG FRANK: No. Mantovani.

YOUNG URSE: No, it's not. Is it?

YOUNG FRANK: No. It's Eddie Condon.

URSULA: You weren't the easiest boys to make advances to.

YOUNG FRANK: How's life among the common folk?

IVOR: The salt of the earth?

YOUNG URSE: How d'you know what it's like where I live? You never come

YOUNG FRANK: Don't want to.

FRANK: I was too frightened. Alone with you on your home ground! You might have found out how little I knew.

YOUNG FRANK: Some of the common folk might breathe on me and give me a disease.

IVOR: They're the sort of people when they go to the pictures think it's all acted on the roof of the cinema and reflected down on to the screen by mirrors.

YOUNG URSE: They don't!

IVOR: I argued with one of them. I said, "D'you really think all those cowboys and Indians are charging across the roof of the Metropole-de-Luxe three or four times a day?" He said, " 'Course they are." I said, "I bet you a month's sweet ration if you nip outside while the film's on, you won't see a single horse or Indian falling off the roof into Lower Osborne Road."

YOUNG URSE: What did he say then?

IVOR: Hit me in the belly-button.

YOUNG FRANK: That's how they finish every discussion the plebs.

IVOR: I shouted, "Brawn versus Brain," but he was half-way back to his slum by then.

(*He and* YOUNG FRANK *laugh and jeer.*)

YOUNG URSE: Got any maths homework?

YOUNG FRANK: Got some simultaneous equations for Thursday.

YOUNG URSE: Easy. Do yours if you do my composition.

YOUNG FRANK: Long as it's not "How I Became So Dirty" by a telephone directory.

YOUNG URSE (*laughing*): My English teacher's not like that. She always gives us something sexy. This week it's "My Ideal Birthday Party".

(*Record finishes.* YOUNG FRANK *takes off arm, shuts door.*)
Shall I tell you what I'd like and you can say it in wizard English?

IVOR: Hellish boring.

(YOUNG FRANK *sits.*)

41

YOUNG URSE (*ignoring him*): I should like all the best-looking boys to come to it and each of them to have a girl except you. And we should play sardines and I'd be hiding in the Anderson shelter and you'd find me straight away.

FRANK (*admiring*): You were so *rude*!

YOUNG URSE: And all the others would give up looking and I'd be your prisoner.

YOUNG FRANK: Better not put that.

YOUNG URSE: Why not?

YOUNG FRANK: Get kicked out.

(*She smiles, takes his hand.*)

YOUNG URSE: How you getting on with School Certificate?

YOUNG FRANK: Okay in French, English and History.

IVOR: That'll be enough to get you into the Civil Service. Make your old man happy.

YOUNG URSE: Mummy says I've got to matriculate as a present for Daddy when he comes home. I hope to get credits or distinctions in Maths, Art and General Science, but it looks as though I'll only get a pass in English. (*She sits on his lap.*)

IVOR: We're not bothering.

YOUNG URSE: You're no good at school anyway. Only art.

IVOR: What good's School Certificate to a film director?

FRANK (*scornfully*): Film director!

IVOR: Frank and I are going into films.

FRANK: Ten years later I had to slog away for A levels in the evenings. As a first step to getting my external degree.

YOUNG URSE: Frank's father thinks you bring him down.

YOUNG FRANK: We know that. "You want to drop that crackpot Ivor, boy——"

IVOR (*imitating*): "He's beyond my comprehension."

YOUNG FRANK: Show her your drawing of our parents, Ive.

(IVOR *takes drawing from pocket, shows* URSE.)

IVOR: My parents and Fran's at one of their hellish boring bridge parties. There's old Amy puffing a Craven A and old Charles coughing his way through the terrific cloud of smoke with a great load of Black Market sweets for my mum. My mum's false teeth have got stuck on a toffee and she's trying desperately to hold them in and with the other hand reaching for another bag. And there's my old man pretending to read the rules of Bridge but really it's a picture of a wore.

(*Pause.* YOUNG URSE *looks at the picture.*)

YOUNG URSE: A what?

IVOR: A wore. That pin-up girl in bra and panties.

YOUNG URSE: W*h*ore, isn't it, Fran?

YOUNG FRANK (*thinking*): Dunno.

IVOR: *Wore* it is.

YOUNG FRANK: No, hang on. I remember the blackmailed wreck reading it aloud——

YOUNG URSE: Who's the blackmailed wreck?

YOUNG FRANK: Our English master. Now I think of it, you must be right, Urse.

"Thou rascal beadle, hold thy bloody hand,
  Why dost thou lash what w*h*ore? Strip thine own back——"

YOUNG URSE: "King Lear"—terrific!

YOUNG FRANK: "Thou hotly lusts to use her in that sport——"

YOUNG URSE: Kind. "That kind for which thou whipst her."

YOUNG FRANK: Yeah.

(*Pause.* IVOR *moves away, folding up his picture.*)

IVOR: I might do a whole great series of these.

YOUNG URSE: Hey, half past four! I've got to get my mother's tea by the time she's home from the factory. (*She prepares to go.*)

URSULA: Making bombers and getting a decent wage for the first time.

YOUNG URSE: You'll do my composition?

YOUNG FRANK: I'll give you my algebra downstairs.

FRANK: And your father was in North Africa.

URSULA: Yes. The government had found him a job at last. After keeping him out of work for most of the thirties.

FRANK: Whatever did he think he was defending—the right to be on the dole?

URSULA: Oh, the poor are always more patriotic in every country. Only the rich are international. Our rich had made friends with Hitler before and they'd have done it again if we'd lost. But we'd have been in labour camps.

43

FRANK: We didn't know that at the time. All we had was Churchill's word for it.

URSULA: Surely he didn't say much about that. A lot about Going Forward Together.

FRANK: That's funny, too, from a man who knew so little about us he'd never even travelled on a 'bus. (*To audience.*) Never once!

URSULA: "We shall fight in the fields," he said, and a lot of people who'd hardly *seen* a field suddenly felt they were the Yeomen of England. Imagine him in my mother's lounge.

FRANK (*imitating Churchill*): As I look around me at this humble hearth . . . the chair of uncut moquette . . . the wireless shaped like an Aztec temple . . . the Polyfoto of the absent father in uniform . . . the years fall away. I see another Agincourt . . . another Waterloo.

URSULA: We all thought he was lovely, though.

FRANK: I remember hating him when he came to inspect our officer material in the Training Corps at school and the rest of us had to stand and cheer and I didn't get home in time to hear the Radio Rhythm Club. And as for understanding what he represented——

URSULA: Nobody in our circles understood anything. That was left to the Brains Trust. We took what pleasure we could and hoped for more later.

FRANK: You got more than I did.

URSULA: Whose fault's that?

FRANK: I know.

URSULA: My mother was far more strict than yours and Uncle frightened the life out of me and my brother. Whereas your father was away half the time and your mother let you do as you liked.

FRANK: None the less there were pleasures, never to be equalled! Listening to jazz. Imitating our elders.

URSULA: I could never keep a straight face in your house. Didn't dare sip my tea in case one of you made me laugh.

FRANK: You liked the old man, didn't you? I was completely mystified by that.

URSULA: Remember mine was away. I think I envied your Friday-to-Monday father cropping up at week-ends——

FRANK: Telling us to take our elbows off the table——

URSULA: Switching all the lights off to leave us stranded in pitch-dark upstairs bathrooms.

FRANK: Coming home a day too soon and interrupting us just as I was about to remove your gym-slip.

URSULA: I'll never quite forgive him for that.

FRANK: You'll never forgive him! I went into the army soon afterwards and had to spend the next three years staring at Chinese and Indian whores and wondering what they did.

URSULA: Years I'd been trying with you.

FRANK: I never guessed. I saw myself as skinny boy on the beach in the Charles Atlas advert.

URSULA: Somehow Ivor was always there too. And that meant sneering because I couldn't tell the Marx Brothers from the Ink Spots. Sometimes you'd chase me into an air-raid shelter in the park but you always rushed back to the safety of the gang before any more could happen.

FRANK: Oh, Christ, those years we lost before the flesh of your thighs collapsed and the whites of my eyes turned red!

URSULA: After you went, I began meeting wartime servicemen just coming home. Men in their twenties who'd been to Greece and Port Said and Berlin.

FRANK: No wonder you've lost interest *now*!

(*She folds her arms impatiently as she sees an old argument coming.*)

No wonder it's "I don't mind as long as we have the light out," or "Quick then before I drop off. . . ."

URSULA: What are you talking about? That's over. We're separated. (*To Audience.*) He left me with three growing children.

FRANK: But I'm remembering . . . reminding myself of the reality of our marriage. You seemed to be able to take it or leave it.

URSULA (*shakes head*): I sometimes want it just as much as you.

FRANK: Too much too young, that's your trouble.

URSULA: Too little too late. Why dwell on it?

FRANK: Because I can't help it. Still emotionally in that back-

45

room, my mind a collage of pin-ups, craving the promiscuity you had and I missed.

URSULA: I wasn't promiscuous in fact——

FRANK: Come on——

URSULA: —not for long, anyway——

FRANK: —ah!——

URSULA (*to Audience*): Only long enough to discover I don't like being treated as just a body.

(FRANK *approaches behind and embraces her. She wearily removes his arms.*)

FRANK: And I've always had this terrible misgiving that women are only after my mind.

URSULA: You've got your chance. You're free. With three dependant kids, no man's going to bother, I'll have to make do with memories.

(*Goes towards door.*)

FRANK: Easy for you——

(*She shuts door behind her. He shouts.*)

—with memories stretching back to the Year One! (*Returns to Audience.*) Memories of meadows . . . sand-dunes . . . innumerable divans . . . the upper decks of buses . . . once, even, she told me, a wing of the Bodleian Library. (*Moves distractedly.*) But mine! Please!

(*The* CHINESE ILLUSIONIST *from the concert party enters without make-up but wearing a cheap silk Chinese kimono. He is smoking a cigarette.*)

MR. MAGIC: I think it's so important to wear the proper clothes for anything, don't you, Frank? Even in our early lessons, before we go to the Baths, it's best to get the feel.

(YOUNG FRANK *comes on in swimming trunks, with vest.*)

And so few boys do what you tell them, d'you know that? (*He makes the cigarette disappear, then reappear.* YOUNG FRANK *stares.*)

I've had boys working for me. Some of my assistants. Neither use nor ornament really. I'm not saying I'm not fond of them, they're sweet boys at heart, but you're all the same, aren't you, full of mischief. (*Takes cigarette from* FRANK's *ear.*)

46

YOUNG FRANK: That's terrific, that. I'm just learning but it's hellish hard.

MR. MAGIC: You stay and work with me, Frank, I'll teach you all the tricks you've ever seen. And quite a few you haven't. (*Throws cigarette into the air and it disappears.*)

FRANK: A sad old queen.

MR. MAGIC: You lack technique, that's all.

FRANK: Well, old? I suppose he was a bit older than I am now.

MR. MAGIC: And I'm only down here in the West because I want to do my bit. Soon as the peace comes, I'll be up in London again. Next time you're there, you mention my name to any of the impresarios in Cambridge Circus. They'll say, "There's no finer artiste in the business than Li Chang."

FRANK: Alias Mister Magic, alias Walter Chambers——

MR. MAGIC: Never anything cheap and nasty——

FRANK: Described as a magician, of no fixed abode——

MR. MAGIC: Never anything artistically degrading, like some you see, with their half-naked tarty girls, their great chests bulging out.

FRANK: Sentenced to six months——

MR. MAGIC: Nothing to turn your stomach. (*He sits.*) We'll have to think of a name for you. Wun Hung Lo. How's that? (YOUNG FRANK *looks cold.*)
Uncle's only joking. What about this breast stroke?

FRANK: No.

MR. MAGIC: Come and sit here.
(*Holds out hand towards him.* YOUNG FRANK *approaches and* MR. MAGIC *sits him on his knee. He looks awkward.*)
Can you swim at all?

YOUNG FRANK: No.

MR. MAGIC: Float?
(YOUNG FRANK *shakes his head.*)
Let's start with floating. Your mother knows where you are, I suppose.

YOUNG FRANK: She knows we're rehearsing, yes. She's gone to my gran's this evening.

MR. MAGIC: Now imagine yourself on the surface of the water. Completely relaxed.

47

FRANK (*moving quickly, dismissing them*): No more!
(YOUNG FRANK *looks at him, then jumps from* MR. MAGIC's *lap and runs off by the door he came from.* MR. MAGIC *moves and calls after him.*)

MR. MAGIC: Frank! Whatever's the matter? What a strange boy you are! Honestly!

FRANK: Get off, get out! (*Shutting his eyes as though to dismiss the thought.*)

MR. MAGIC (*to him*): Don't you shout at me. You can't push people out as easily as that!

FRANK: Can't I!
(*Moves swiftly towards him.* MR. MAGIC *goes, leaving open door, which* FRANK *slams and holds shut.* MR. MAGIC *opens door near by.*)

MR. MAGIC: All your life you'll be wincing at the memory.
(FRANK *leaves door, runs to shut him out again. Sound of footsteps continues behind wall and* FRANK *follows the sound until it stops on opposite side of stage. He waits for the door to open. It doesn't. He opens it wide. Nobody there.* MR. MAGIC *opens the door by which he first went out.*)
I'm part of your mental landscape for ever, duckie, whether you like it or——
(FRANK *runs to the door and slams him out. Laugh behind wall.* FRANK *returns to front.*)

FRANK: I ran home in the summer evening, frightened and mystified. I thought only boys did that and then only until they could find a girl. But why men? And old heavy-breathing men with brown teeth. I passed some girls with great chests bulging out which far from turned my stomach. Ursula was waiting with the rest of our crowd in the local park but first I had to collect some cigarettes I'd stolen from Dad and hidden up my bedroom chimney. But I was not to be let off so easily, there was more bewildering unpleasantness to come. He appeared in a cloud of steam from the bathroom as I climbed the stairs and insisted I take over his water. "I've used rather more than the regulation five inches, boy, and we should help the war effort any way we can." The bathroom was exhausted, the walls

48

sweating, the soap melting in the high humidity. And while I lay in this warm soup, he pottered about from room to room, gradually dressing.

(CHARLES *comes on, wearing open shirt without collar and trousers but with bare feet. Around his neck is a towel and he is reading a book. He speaks to* YOUNG FRANK *offstage.*)

CHARLES: Cleanliness is next to godliness. I shall always remember my mother saying that.

FRANK: As soon as possible, I rubbed down and pulled on my trousers.

CHARLES: And we had no bathrooms in those days, boy, only a hip-bath before the fire and a clothes-horse round with towels hung over it.

(*Opens a door which has clothes and shoes behind it, a wardrobe. He takes out pair of slippers and pair of shoes, then consults the book. He returns the left slipper and the right shoe to the wardrobe, leaving door open.*)

I recall one night my brother saying to Sister Emma, "Don't come in when one of us boys is in the bath, Sis. You never know what we may be a-doing-of."

(*He laughs at the thought, he puts on the slipper and the shoe, consults the book again and rolls up his left trouser-leg, sitting on chair level to do so. Hears movement off. Goes to side, looking off.*)

You out? Bring the *Reynolds News* from the attic stairway, will you, Son?

FRANK: Later on Ivor taught me swimming in the public baths with an inflatable belt.

(CHARLES *opens another door to reveal shelves full of patent medicines and toilet preparations in jars, bottles, tubes and tins.*)

Ten years of samples. Friar's Balsam, Cascara, Vapour Rub, Golden Eye Ointment. It was among his boasts that he never recommended any line he hadn't personally tested.

(CHARLES *takes down bottle, wad of cotton wool and nail-scissors.* YOUNG FRANK *comes on, wearing trousers, shirt and tie, no shoes or socks. He carries a newspaper.*)

CHARLES (*taking paper*): It's Brother Edwin about whom I'm

D   49

talking. Used to frighten the life out of Sister Emma.
(*Places medicines, etc., on raised surface, spreads paper on floor by seat.* YOUNG FRANK *continues tying his tie.*)

D'you know his term for the convenience, Frank?

YOUNG FRANK: The Gold Mine.

CHARLES: He used to call it The Gold Mine.
(*Laughs.* YOUNG FRANK *looks at his eccentric clothes, shrugs and starts to go as* CHARLES *turns to him.*)

Buzfuz!

YOUNG FRANK: What?

CHARLES: What's "what"?

YOUNG FRANK: What is it?

CHARLES: "What is it, *Dad*?"

YOUNG FRANK: I'm just off out.

CHARLES: Where are you going, Son?

YOUNG FRANK: Meeting Ivor in the park.

CHARLES: And what's that round your neck?

YOUNG FRANK: A dragon tie. Ivor painted it. The dragon's luminous.

CHARLES: What a way to dress!

YOUNG FRANK: What about *you*! What's your trouser rolled up for?

CHARLES: For what is your trouser rolled up?
(*Pause. He realizes this is not quite right yet.*)

YOUNG FRANK (*smiles*): Up for what is your trouser rolled?

CHARLES: Don't talk big, you make yourself look small.

YOUNG FRANK: Why one slipper and one shoe?

CHARLES: If I'm doing it, Son, you can bet there's a jolly proper reason. I wouldn't walk through the streets like it, any more than I'd wear a luminous dragon tie and chase young Ursula and her friends in and out of the air-raid shelters.

YOUNG FRANK: Who said we do?

CHARLES: Mister Lewthwaite lives beside the park overlooking the static water tank. He can see you from his bedroom window.

YOUNG FRANK: I'll bet he's up there every night with b-b-b-binoculars.

CHARLES: I hear you making fun of anyone's afflictions, you'll feel the back of my hand.

YOUNG FRANK: *You* do it!

CHARLES: Don't answer back.

YOUNG FRANK: You're always doing it. You always call him tah-tah-Tiny Lewthwaite.

CHARLES: Mister Lewthwaite's an influential man these days. Chief Buyer in Fancy Goods. And what's more, a Master Mason. He's sponsoring me for admission to his lodge. And that's why I'm dressed like this, you great coon.
(*He has approached* YOUNG FRANK *and seized his ear.*)
How long since you cleaned your ears out?
(YOUNG FRANK *groans.* CHARLES *peers in.*)
By Jove!
(*Takes handkerchief from pocket, folds and twists it into a flexible spike.* YOUNG FRANK *finishes tie and makes to go.*)
Stand still when I tell you.
(*Holds* FRANK'*s head, plunges spike into one ear.*)

YOUNG FRANK: Ow!

CHARLES: Don't jerk away.

YOUNG FRANK: You'll break my eardrum. V'you got a matchstick in that hankie?

CHARLES: Don't be absurd.

YOUNG FRANK: You had last time. Nearly deafened me for life.

CHARLES: I wonder you're not deaf already. Enough wax here to furnish Madame Tussauds.

YOUNG FRANK (*breaking away*): Hey, shut up!

CHARLES: Shurrup? What's shurrup? If I'd spoken like that to my father, I'd have felt the back of his hand.

YOUNG FRANK: You're not going to hold him up as an example, are you? A drunkard.
(*He has moved away and* CHARLES *sits down, cutting his toenails into the newspaper.*)

CHARLES: Yes, and when he was drunk, he couldn't move very fast, he couldn't see to hit us. We boys got pretty nimble dodging his fists. He used to shout: "Come here, you little b-u-double-g-a-r!"

YOUNG FRANK: *E*-r.

51

CHARLES: Pardon?

YOUNG FRANK: B-u-double-g-*e*-r.

CHARLES: How d'you know?

YOUNG FRANK: I've seen it written on walls.

FRANK: In conveniences.

CHARLES: You shouldn't *read* it! You must develop the habit of turning away from smut in any size, shape or form. D'you think as a grocery traveller I haven't had to wrestle with temptation?

FRANK: I felt he was leading somewhere.

CHARLES: D'you think my colleagues in commercial hotels don't hang about the lounge-bars swapping smut? They sometimes say, "Come along, Charles, be social, have a lemonade shandy with us," and I look into the bar and smell the booze and see the landlord drawing ale and d'you know what always comes to me, Son?

YOUNG FRANK: The words of——

CHARLES: The words of Shakespeare, "How like a fawning publican he looks!"
(*Goes on cutting toenails into paper.* YOUNG FRANK *waits, checking appearance in mirror.*)

FRANK: A better line was Lady Macbeth's. "All the perfumes of Arabia will not sweeten this little hand."

CHARLES (*standing*): Get a bottle of wintergreen, I'll rub some into your legs.

YOUNG FRANK: I don't want that terrific pongy stuff wherever I go.

CHARLES: I'll empty these clippings out the window. Do the garden good.
(*Shakes newspaper over audience, folds and puts on seat.*)
And women, too, on the road. Normally decent but after a few gins, they make their loins available. These are bad times, Frank, you've been going round entertaining, you've met girls whose conduct isn't quite what it should be, I dare say. (*Fetches bandage from cupboard and begins binding ankle.*)

FRANK: Had he heard about my hand beneath the dancer's thighs? Say something!

YOUNG FRANK: Why d'you put that bandage round your leg?

52

CHARLES: You surely know already. My varicose veins?

YOUNG FRANK (*innocent*): No.

FRANK: Only too well.

CHARLES: During the First World War, as I was due for military service. Months in hospital, a hundred stitches. That—together with the deafness caused by that clout across the ear—saved me from the trenches, so I'm not sorry. If the war's still on when you're eighteen, you may get out with bed-wetting.

YOUNG FRANK: I'd rather go to the war than wet the bed.

CHARLES: That shows a very decent spirit. But use your savvy, there are always plenty of piecans prepared to fight.

YOUNG FRANK: Your veins must be all right now. Why d'you still wear the bandage?

CHARLES: Nobody's ever told me to stop. Besides, it keeps my ankles cosy.

(YOUNG FRANK *grins*.)

FRANK (*praying*): "Ursula, please wait for me, I'm coming as soon as I can get away."

CHARLES: Well, while you're so busy reading smut on the walls of conveniences, perhaps you could spare a glance for the Ministry of Health's announcement about g-o-n-o-r-h, no, double-r-h-e-a, no——

YOUNG FRANK: Double-r h-o-e-a.

FRANK: I could spell anything.

CHARLES: Your mother and I have never interfered, only tried to set an example of clean living. You follow me?

YOUNG FRANK: Okay. Going to see Ivor now.

CHARLES: Wait a jiffy. Before you go out fondling young Ursula, you can help——

YOUNG FRANK: I'm seeing Ivor!

CHARLES: Don't tell me fibs, Son. I called at Ivor's on the way home with a pound of bacon for his father. They're all going to his aunt's for the evening. Now tell me honestly, Son, where are you going?

YOUNG FRANK: The park.

CHARLES: To fondle young Ursula?

YOUNG FRANK: No.

FRANK: If her mother got to hear of it, she'd keep her in.

YOUNG FRANK: Honestly.

CHARLES: You tell me honestly, boy, I believe you.
(*Stands and faces him.* YOUNG FRANK *looks at his feet.*)
Do your finger-nails need cutting?

YOUNG FRANK: No. (*Turns to go.*)

CHARLES: Your toenails?

YOUNG FRANK: No. (*Turns to go again.*)

CHARLES: What's the hurry? Here, take this book. I'm trying to learn the ceremonial.

YOUNG FRANK: What for?

CHARLES: My initiation. Once all the applications have gone through and no one rules me out, I get the call, you see.

YOUNG FRANK (*reading book*): It says you've got to surrender all your money.

CHARLES: I've left it on the chest of drawers, all five and eight-pence halfpenny. It's so that when in future I meet a Mason needing help, I call to mind the day I was received, poor and penniless.

YOUNG FRANK: You get the money back afterwards?

CHARLES: Well, what d'you think, you great pudden?

YOUNG FRANK: It's all a fake then.

CHARLES: The entire movement of freemasonry a fake? You're going to set yourself up in opposition to all the great men who've believed in it, are you?

YOUNG FRANK: What great men? Tiny Lewthwaite?

CHARLES: Mozart, Sir Christopher Wren, George Washington, Frederick the Great, Garibaldi, our present King. Percy Tombs.

YOUNG FRANK: Who?

CHARLES: Mister Tombs, Grocery Manager for the whole South-West division. He's the Worshipful Master of the Lodge.

YOUNG FRANK: You're supposed to be blindfold.

CHARLES: Hoodwinked, yes. (*He has his handkerchief ready, blindfolds himself.*)

YOUNG FRANK: And wear a noose round your neck.

CHARLES: You haven't a handy length of rope?

YOUNG FRANK: No.

CHARLES: We'll take it as read. Now. The Tyler escorts me to the threshold and the Inner Guard, his dagger to my bare breast, leads me before the Worshipful Master. He asks certain ritual questions, the answers to which I mean to commit to memory.

FRANK: But his memory was as cluttered as mine is now.

CHARLES: With my gift of the gab, I should find no difficulty responding in a loud clear voice like a sergeant-major. Then —with my right foot formed in a square—I kneel before the Worshipful Master.

YOUNG FRANK: Percy Tombs.

CHARLES (*kneeling*): Mister Tombs. And swear not to reveal—um —what is it, Sonny Jim?

YOUNG FRANK: Write, indite, carve, mark, engrave or otherwise delineate——

(CHARLES *has repeated these words quietly after him.*)

CHARLES: The secrets of Masonry, yes. These are the bits I must get off pat.

YOUNG FRANK: On pain of having your throat cut across, your tongue torn out by the root and buried in the sand of the sea at low water mark—or a cable's length from the shore. Can't wait to tell old Ivor this.

CHARLES (*sitting back on heels*): You what? You dare, boy!

YOUNG FRANK: To think of old Tiny Lewthwaite doing this terrific Bela Lugosi act——

CHARLES: Not so much of the jolly old buck! The disrespect.

YOUNG FRANK: Well, it's so hellish corny.

CHARLES: It's dashed easy for you to sneer, boy, you're not away from home Monday to Friday wondering how to fill the time in draughty commercial hotels. You're not standing around in God-forsaken grocery departments awaiting the pleasure of foul-mouthed branch managers, swallowing their insults, laughing at their smut. D'you think I like that?

YOUNG FRANK: Dunno.

CHARLES: Dunno? What's dunno? No's the answer.

FRANK: I used to wonder how he would have managed in the army.

CHARLES: Any more than Mister Lewthwaite liked it. And how

did he get a job at H.Q.? When did he move from traveller to buyer? Six months after joining the Masonic Lodge.

YOUNG FRANK: Okay, I'm going out——

CHARLES: Listen till I've finished. How am I else to get promotion, bring myself to the attention of the powers-that-be?

FRANK: I felt he was leading somewhere. But where?

CHARLES: Mister Tombs is one of those powers, boy. A very big cheese in the grocery trade. And a Worshipful Master.

YOUNG FRANK: Be getting dark soon——

CHARLES (*suddenly seizing his hands*): Where you off to, eh?

YOUNG FRANK: The park, I told you.

(*Moves slightly, pulling* CHARLES *so that he has to move on his knees. Strengthens his grip on* FRANK.)

CHARLES: Going to your mother, Son?

YOUNG FRANK: Eh?

CHARLES: Have you said you'd meet your mother?

YOUNG FRANK: No. She's at Gran's place.

CHARLES: That's where she *says* she is. But you know more than I do, you're here all the week. She *says* she's spending all this time at her mother's but—do you think she is, Son?

YOUNG FRANK: Why not?

CHARLES: You know.

FRANK: I didn't *know*. It was the first I'd heard of it.

(YOUNG FRANK *tries to go again.*)

CHARLES: Frank, don't go to her!

YOUNG FRANK: I'm not.

CHARLES: You're not seeing Ivor, you're not seeing Ursula, then where *are* you going if not to her? Listen, Son, if your mother left me, would you go with her? Please, Frank, if she goes . . . she might ask you to choose between us, you see what I mean, boy . . . well, look, stay with me, there's a good boy. Remember all I've done for you.

(FRANK *turns away, wincing at the memory.*)

YOUNG FRANK (*frightened*): Going to the park——

CHARLES: Given you an education, put you by a nest-egg . . .

(YOUNG FRANK *stands, looking away.*)

. . . there's more in my will, if I don't change my mind.

FRANK (*wincing*): I'm not sure he said that.

56

CHARLES: Frank!

FRANK: But he might have, which is all that matters.

CHARLES: I've had to be strict, coming home as I do at week-ends
—and sometimes perhaps I seemed *too* strict—but it's all
very well for your mother to spoil you . . . I don't seem able
to talk to you.

YOUNG FRANK: All right.

(*Stands for a long time.*)

CHARLES: Don't be late.

YOUNG FRANK: No.

(*Goes quickly,* CHARLES *unrolls his trouser leg, still kneeling.*)

FRANK: More than anything, I've inherited his sexual nature.
Inasmuch as I understand it. A lack of mastery. Dependence.
I suppose leaving my wife was an effort not to repeat the
pattern.

(*Shakes head.* CHARLES *blows nose in handkerchief, wipes face.*)
But I'm afraid I shall weaken in the end. Ursula can manage,
she'll survive. She'd never beg, but I would. A few months of
this loneliness will see me on my knees. (*He turns to look at*
CHARLES. *To him.*) I didn't mention it to her. Never mentioned those two encounters to anyone. Not even Ivor.

(CHARLES *doesn't seem to hear. He stands, puts away slipper*
and shoe.)
That should give you some satisfaction.

(CHARLES *shuts door.* FRANK *turns to audience.*)
Conveniently deaf. But it's true.

(CHARLES *goes off taking newspaper.*)
I was so keen to find Ursula that I at once forgot those mani-
festations of the male menopause. Didn't remember them
again till years later. The church clock showed half past eight
as I free-wheeled past the water-tank and glimpsed our crowd
lounging by the shelters. For twenty minutes we jeered at
each other and groaned with derision at the girls' stupidity.
Now and then there was a chase in and out of the shelters
and Ursula could always find me inside by my quietly glow-
ing dragon. Then a sudden sound, a shouting of orders, some
cheers and the beautiful silver barrage balloon lurched up
behind the bandstand. It had broken moorings and was now

carried away over the rooftops . . . and giggling Waafs in battledress pursued it through the streets to mark where it fell. More than enough to make you forget your family— that great shining whale racing on the evening breeze! (*Shuts his eyes, pulls himself back to the present, looks about, then at his wrist-watch.*) Time to go for a bite. (*Goes to door, opens it, pauses in opening. Then goes on to Audience, as actor.*) If you'd like a drink, there are several bars you can go to.

(*Another door opens and* YOUNG FRANK *appears.*)

YOUNG FRANK (*imitating* CHARLES): What's "you can go to", you great coon?

IVOR (*appearing at another, also imitates*): To which you can go, boy——

YOUNG FRANK ⎱
IVOR ⎰ To which you can go.

CHARLES (*at another*): Don't talk so big, you make yourself look small.

AMY (*at another*): Oh, do stop going on at the boy.

MR. MAGIC (*at another*): Boy! That was a long time ago and through a gauze!

FRANK: Can't you leave me alone for ten minutes!

(*They all slam doors together.*)

ACT TWO

Another record recital in the break:
    The Day War Broke Out *by Robb Wilton.*
    Don't Get Around Much Any More *by Duke Ellington.*
    Room 504 *by Hutch.*
    Milkman, Keep Those Bottles Quiet *by Andrews Sisters.*
    High Society *by Bob Crosby.*
    Towards the end, FRANK *comes in finishing a newspaper of fish and chips, stands listening to the record. Eats last chip, screws up paper, discards in bin below record-player. Wipes hands on handkerchief. He runs the tape forward at high speed, then stops it to play a personal recording. Thus:*

FRANK: Now, Matthew, say hullo.
BOY: No.
FRANK: All right.
BOY: Don't want to.
FRANK: Why not?
    (*Silence, then sounds of microphone moved, a great crackle.*)
    No, don't touch it. Don't put it in your mouth. You never know where it's been.
    (*Laugh from* URSULA.)
URSULA: Tell Daddy what you did in school today, Jenny.
GIRL: Wrote about you.
URSULA: Me?
GIRL: And Daddy.
FRANK: What did you say about me?
GIRL: What you looked like.
FRANK: You mean old and grey?

59

GIRL: I said you don't look as old as you really are.
(URSULA *laughs*.)

FRANK: That's right. Spread the word. And how about an explosive remark or two from our representative of permissiveness, teen-age protest and any other rubbish that's going?
(*Pause*.)

URSULA (*quietly*): What an invitation! I don't know how you could resist it, Bill.
(BILL, FRANK's *elder son, is played by same actor as Young Frank*.)

BILL: Really great. Okay. This is William Bisley, aged fourteen, making his contribution to this grotty recording . . . which is meant to give an impression of a typical evening at home . . . but is actually about as natural as a school photograph. Can I go now?

FRANK: Thank you. That should certainly stir them up in Grosvenor Square. Certainly get them charging the police horses.

URSULA: Frank! Why do you——
(*Voice fades away. Mike noises again. Then voices recorded at a faster speed. Then* FRANK, URSULA *and the younger children singing "A Song of Sixpence".* FRANK *leaves it playing, goes off, returns at end with a glass of milk. Stares again at recorder. After the song,* FRANK *and* URSULA *tell the children how well they sang*.)

FRANK (*on tape*): Now shall we listen to that?
(FRANK *switches it off, closes door, comes down, drinking*.)
Is the family inevitable? Even our religion is based on a family—and with *two* fathers. I always identify with Joseph, the best-known victim of *droit de seigneur* . . . sawing away out the back while angels are streaming in and out of the bedroom window.

Is it natural? If it is, I am a freak because I failed. You haven't failed. You looked at your family steadily for some time, saw what it was doing to all its members and decided rationally to dismantle it.

When we're kids we don't really question the adult

world, just blunder about in a jungle of meaningless rules. But at twelve or so, confused by erections and periods, armed with the pure logic of puberty, we start fighting in earnest. Which scares our parents and sets up conflict. School drones on and on: French verbs and wanker's doom. Then at last—escape, freedom! Lovely to start with but after all we need a regular cuddle at nights and there's no other way but a family of our own choice. One without rules. Paradise. But before we know it, most of our time's spent dabbing snot, healing greedy screams with ice-lolly . . . saying do this, don't do that . . . our wives, who were sex-pots a minute ago, are nagging shrews from a seaside postcard. (*Finishes milk, puts glass down.*)

Our girl Jenny, at three, already took profound pleasure in organization, bullying her dolls, lining them up, smacking her teddies and being motherly. When Matthew was born, of course, and began to grow, she set him down amongst the teddies and nagged him, for all the world as though they were married. I used to watch him dreaming through it all and in the end he'd crawl away and she'd come howling that he'd spoilt the game. Our lives are an extrapolation of infancy— termagant girls and dreamy boys. Then, of course, infants are imitating adults. So how do you break the circle? Well, I'm trying.

(*Pause, then he moves again.*)

For years I couldn't face these facts. Sometimes I'd stand for minutes while the abuse poured over my head like hailstones, then I'd go, slamming the door, longing for a brainstorm that never came, thinking I'd failed, resentful and ashamed at the same time. Then one day, we had a screaming match over —I can't even remember now—the position of an armchair. And she said, "I can't stand much more of this," and I said, "Nor can I. I've thought about it, too. I'll go." And I looked seriously at the thought of life without her, after fourteen years. Miserable—but perhaps that was what life required of me.

(URSULA *has come on quietly and is listening.*)

To take on the loneliness of bachelor life again. But with the

loneliness a freedom too . . . from family car-trips, children's
telly, Wellington boots . . . fish-fingers. . . .

URSULA: If you loved your children, you'd accept all that.
(*He turns to her.*)

FRANK: I love them.

URSULA: Not enough.

FRANK: What is "enough"? There were times when I thought
them the whole reason for living.

URSULA: Is that why you left home? Because you loved them?

FRANK: No. Because we should break up families.

URSULA: They tried it on the kubbutzim. Most of them have
voted to have the children back.

FRANK: The women. I wonder what the men had to say. And
the children, for that matter. It'll take a couple of genera-
tions to form a proper opinion.

URSULA: And the opinion will be the same: the family's inevitable.

FRANK: Then God help us.

URSULA: And while working out this crappy theory did you ever
consider me? My life afterwards? A woman of—(*Pause*)—
past her best——

FRANK (*to Audience*): Thirty-eight——

URSULA (*glance too, icy smile at him*): Thank you. With three
children.

FRANK: Of course and it kept me with you for years. But you're
tough, Ursula, you're a survivor. Other people tend to say,
"Wait till Ursula comes, she'll know what to do," I knew
you could manage without me far more easily than I——

URSULA: And do you think I *wanted* to be like that?

FRANK: You *were* like that.

URSULA: Because I had to be. With four people depending on
me.

FRANK: That's my point. Without the family, you wouldn't *have*
to be like that. You and I could have chased each other
from room to room. But you spent more time buying
potted geraniums than making love to me.

URSULA: Are we back to this? Who mentioned this? I'm talking
about my life and what I should like to be.

FRANK: Well?

URSULA: I'd like to do what you do. Sit about all day with a lot of students and set the world to rights.

FRANK: Fine. It's never too late. But in the time you used to spend cooking, gardening, fruit-bottling, washing nappies, ironing, taking to school and bringing back, playing Old Maid——

URSULA: All right, I know how I fill the day.

FRANK: In the time you used to spend doing that, you could surely have spared an afternoon in the bedroom.

URSULA: Oh, Frank.

FRANK: Notice: afternoon. Not night, when you're dying to get to sleep, or morning when you're in a hurry to get them dressed for school. But—before we had them, you were so exciting.

URSULA: You're jealous of them.

FRANK: I think I had cause.

URSULA: It's your age. You remember it as better than it was.

FRANK: I remember.

(*Opens door to pin-up collage.*)

You were what my grandma used to call a brazen hussy.

(YOUNG FRANK *comes on wearing 1945 utility casuals, with* YOUNG URSE *in school uniform, carrying satchel.*)

YOUNG FRANK: How d'you get off hockey?

YOUNG URSE: Forged an excuse-note.

URSULA: I was a clever counterfeiter. I used to forge everyone's notes.

(YOUNG URSE *drops satchel, takes off raincoat.*)

FRANK: Excited, breathless, gratified, but wishing I'd never asked you.

(YOUNG FRANK *yawns.*)

URSULA: Scared as a rabbit with a snake, wondering when you'd start.

YOUNG URSE: Your mum's out?

YOUNG FRANK: Pictures. And Dad's in Worcester.

(*She sits.*)

YOUNG URSE: Your holiday's nearly over.

YOUNG FRANK (*nods*): Go next week.

63

YOUNG URSE: You frightened?

YOUNG FRANK: Glad to be getting away from this dump. With Ivor gone and everything . . .

FRANK: He'd been called up a few months before.

YOUNG URSE: Have you heard from him again?

YOUNG FRANK: Nearly finished square-bashing. Sent some terrific drawings of the plebs. He says quite a few of them can't even read the comics. Blokes of eighteen and twenty can't even read!

YOUNG URSE: Hellish dim.

(*He stands by her, yawns again. She stretches her legs out in front of her, looks at them. Then she takes his hand.*)

Hullo, Handsome.

YOUNG FRANK: Oh, Christ!

YOUNG URSE: What d'you want me to say?

YOUNG FRANK: Hullo, Skinny.

YOUNG URSE: You're not skinny, you're slim.

FRANK (*like someone watching a prize-fight*): Get on with it, man!

YOUNG URSE (*kisses his hand*): I like thin boys.

YOUNG FRANK: Then why've you been going round with that brawny crowd from near the Baths?

URSULA: Because you seemed to prefer Ivor. But when he went I came running back.

YOUNG URSE: They were hellish boring. All they talked about was getting in the air and shooting down Germans and Japs. They never saw it as a film, like you and Ivor.

YOUNG FRANK: "I can't stand any more, I tell you, let me go."

FRANK: "Pull yourself together, for Pete's sake, Jerry's watching."

YOUNG URSE: I like boys who make me laugh.

(*Stands, puts arms round him, kisses him on mouth. He embraces her.*)

URSULA: I deserved a good hiding.

FRANK: You were marvellous, but look at me!

URSULA: When Dad was released, he took me in hand.

(YOUNG URSE *pulls out* YOUNG FRANK's *shirt. He yawns.*)

YOUNG URSE: You tired?

(*He shrugs.*)

Let's lie down. Shall we?
(*She sits again.*)
I'm hot. Aren't you? Hellish hot today.
(*He goes on knees and takes off her shoes.*)
URSULA: This isn't nice at all.
FRANK: It's improving.
(YOUNG FRANK *kisses* YOUNG URSE's *knee, then sits by
her.*)
YOUNG URSE: You're terrifically attractive, Frank.
FRANK: Tell her! Tell her she's attractive! Tell her about your
dreams!
(YOUNG FRANK *plays with* YOUNG URSE's *school tie. She waits.
She unties it. He opens a shirt button. She opens one of his.*)
YOUNG URSE: Quite a few hairs since last I looked.
YOUNG FRANK: Four.
FRANK: Mostly grey now.
YOUNG URSE: I cried the other night in bed because I thought
you might not come back.
YOUNG FRANK: Why not?
YOUNG URSE: Might get killed.
YOUNG FRANK: The war's nearly over.
YOUNG URSE: Not in the Far East.
FRANK: The bomb was coming.
YOUNG FRANK: That's mostly the Yanks. They won't send me.
URSULA: But they did.
YOUNG URSE: Shall I wait for you? While you're away.
YOUNG FRANK: Oh. If you like.
FRANK: What eloquence!
YOUNG URSE: I'm fagged out. Shall we lie down?
(*She lies down and he leans over her.*)
URSULA: Why d'you have to dwell on this?
FRANK: You were wonderful.
(YOUNG FRANK *kisses her, then takes something from her
cheek with his finger.*)
YOUNG URSE: What is it?
FRANK: A piece of amalgam.
YOUNG URSE: Silver stuff.
YOUNG FRANK: I had a tooth filled this morning.

FRANK: Remember that?

URSULA: Yes. I kept it in my souvenir box till you came home.
(CHARLES *comes in with case, wearing suit. Shuts door behind him.* YOUNG FRANK *jumps up.*)

YOUNG FRANK: That's the front door.
(YOUNG URSE *gets up.*)

YOUNG URSE: Are you sure?

YOUNG FRANK: Mum must have come home early.

CHARLES (*calling*): Anyone home?
(YOUNG FRANK *and* YOUNG URSE *start dressing rapidly.*)

YOUNG FRANK: Hullo?

FRANK: I knew I had to answer.

URSULA: Why?

FRANK: If he'd thought I was out, he'd have gone to my room to read my diary.

URSULA: Would he really?

FRANK: Yes.

CHARLES: You up there, boy?

YOUNG FRANK (*dressing*): Yes! Coming down.

URSULA: Why?

FRANK: To see what I'd written about him.

URSULA: How d'you know he read it?
(CHARLES *puts his case on a table and opens it, pushing through the papers to find paper bag. From this he takes a half-pound of butter and a packet of tea.*)

FRANK: He couldn't resist correcting what I'd put.

URSULA: "Preposition at end of sentence"?

CHARLES (*shouts*): Come on, noodle!

FRANK: Yes, or once, I remember, I had written: "In a vase on the mantelpiece there is a Remembrance Poppy. Is the old man keeping it till next November to save a shilling?"
(YOUNG FRANK *and* YOUNG URSE *go out one door while* CHARLES *unpacks half-pound of cheese and some biscuits.* YOUNG FRANK *closes pin-up screens.*)
And he added in the margin, "Do not tell untruths or show ingratitude to a father who has shown you every generosity."
(YOUNG FRANK *and* YOUNG URSE *re-enter by same door as* CHARLES.)

YOUNG FRANK: Thought you were in Worcester.

CHARLES: The usual sunny welcome home. Hullo, young woman, are you quite well?

YOUNG URSE: Hullo, Mister Bisley.

CHARLES: What are you a-doing-of upstairs with Sonny Jim? My brother Edwin used to frighten the life out of Sister Emma, you know. He used to say, "Don't come in when the old man is in the bath, Sis. You never know what he might be a-doing-of."

YOUNG FRANK: I been helping her with her schoolwork.

CHARLES: Judging by the showing you made in your exams, she'd be better off without your help.

(YOUNG FRANK *groans*.)

You warm, Ursula? You look warm, your face is flushed. So's yours, boy. Open the window if you're warm. It was sweltering in Tewkesbury.

YOUNG FRANK: Why d'you come back then?

CHARLES: I'd completed all my calls in double-quick time and never one to outstay my welcome, left *tout de suite*, got a jolly old move-on and here I am, in person, the one and only, Charles the First and Foremost. And you can give me a hand unloading one or two samples from the car.

YOUNG FRANK (*taking paper bag from case*): Some samples of fresh eggs here.

CHARLES: Leave them alone. They're a gift. Would your mother like a couple of eggs, Ursula? Naturally. People talk about things improving but in the grocery trade there's little jubilation at the immediate prospect of peace. Mister Lewthwaite of Fancy Goods, a real coon if ever there was one, said to me, "There's massive supplies on the way from America." I looked up at the ceiling, then at the window, then I looked him in the eye and I said, "Oh?" very slowly, you know, boy, that frightens the life out of them.

YOUNG FRANK: Makes them curl up laughing.

CHARLES: I said, "Then am I to assume that you are privy to Mister Attlee's innermost thoughts? Or have you received a p.c. from Mister Truman this a.m.?" Then he started, Ursula, "I sah-sah-sah-," he had a pitiful stammer. I let him struggle for a bit then I went on, "If you believe that the cessation of hostilities—who"—Who said that, cessation of hostilities? I'll give him a kick in the pants.

(*Kicks himself.* URSULA *and* YOUNG URSE *laugh.*)

What are you laughing at, young woman? I said, "If you believe that the cessation of hostilities will result in an immediate and wellnigh torrential flow of milk and honey, you must be an even bigger noodle than I thought. Good morning." I walked off and left him gasping.

YOUNG FRANK: Left him thinking you were hellish corny.

CHARLES: Not so much of the jolly old buck, thank you, from a boy who can't even do up his shirt on the right buttons.

(*Begins unbuttoning* YOUNG FRANK'*s shirt at neck.*)

YOUNG FRANK (*embarrassed*): I can do it.

CHARLES (*continuing to do it*): Hold your tongue.

(YOUNG FRANK *suffers it.*)

URSULA: Touching you again, you see. He always struck me as a very tactile person, for ever trying to touch you. Your mother as well, but you both avoided him.

CHARLES (*to* YOUNG URSE): Your buttons all right, young woman?

(YOUNG URSE *giggles.*)

URSULA: I've always been ashamed of the way we must have appeared to him that day. And me only sixteen!

FRANK: I'll bet his puritan imagination ran riot.

CHARLES: You shouldn't go up to that back room amongst those photographs of uncovered girls. Might give you the wrong ideas, eh, boy. Might start uncovering herself. And if Buzfuz here starts making free with you, send him packing. Take a leaf from my mother's book. If the old man came sniffing round her in his cups, she'd say, "Hands off, private property!" I've heard her.

YOUNG FRANK: No wonder he drank.

CHARLES: Your hair badly wants cutting.

(*Touches* YOUNG FRANK'*s hair. He backs away.*)

URSULA: Touching again.

CHARLES: All curly in your neck. However. Look at that car standing out there. The only car in the avenue, it looks like showing off. Take these things to the kitchen, boy, pending your mother's return from the flicks. And both of you come and help unload. You don't want to sit upstairs, Ursula, giving yourself ideas, getting all flushed.

(YOUNG FRANK *takes packages*, CHARLES *closes suitcase and holds it.* YOUNG URSE *laughs*.)

D'you know this great coon has requested, nay demanded, that the back room shall remain unaltered till he comes home from the army? Just fancy, His Majesty's Government, in their wisdom, have decided he's A1, in the pink and fit to defend our far-flung empire. Especially now he's stopped wetting the bed.

(*Laughs, goes off, followed by* YOUNG URSE, *shyly.* YOUNG FRANK *goes by the other door.*)

FRANK (*shouting at the door by which* CHARLES *left*): Insensitive, pre-Freudian clown!

(*Door opens.* CHARLES *looks in.*)

CHARLES: Don't raise your voice at me, Son.

(FRANK *slams door on him.*)

URSULA: Did he keep the room as it was?

FRANK: Yes.

URSULA: I didn't go there again for years and the pin-up girls had gone by then.

FRANK: You were busy elsewhere.

URSULA: At school and then at college. The Americans went, with terrific scenes at the station, when all the good-time girls turned up with their sepia babies and the train couldn't start. The police finally cleared them out but they stood in the forecourt chanting, "We want our husbands! Give us our husbands!" My dad came home, with all the other men who'd voted Churchill out. He got a well-paid factory job and my brother and I went to college. Life was certainly better for us than before the war. I studied dress-making.

FRANK: Funny name for it.

URSULA: What else would you call it?

FRANK: Dress removing?

URSULA (*understands, decides*): Right. (*She goes to door.*)

69

FRANK: No, love, wait——

(*But she goes, shutting door.*)

Ivor and I never met again till I was released. What my
mother would have called a blessing in disguise. We vowed
to write to each other every week and more or less kept the
promise, but it was like a stale marriage. The crazy gags
and caricatures of our adolescence weren't an adequate
response to what I was seeing now: the end of British India,
the cruelty of Calcutta, Gandhi's death. I knew that sooner
or later I should have to tell him it was finished but suffi-
cient unto the day, as my mother would have said.

(AMY *comes from a door, dressed for 1948, aged 47.*)

AMY: You got home about—what?—half past two. Dad was in
Cardiff so I'd had a spot of dinner on my own, after finish-
ing the spring cleaning in the morning, because I wanted it
looking nice. So I thought, "I'll just sit down for ten
minutes with a cork-tipped," when this knock came and
there you were. (*To Audience.*) Very sun-tanned but thin as a
rake, I thought to myself, I'll soon fatten him up. You'd had
dinner on the train so I said, "How about some tea?" and
you said, "Coffee," you said you'd acquired the taste, and
luckily there was just enough essence in the bottle.

FRANK: Before I'd drunk it, Ivor came on a second-hand motorbike
and I had to struggle to remember our mutual vocabulary.

AMY: You went upstairs with him straight away.

(*Pin-up screens open.* IVOR *comes on, a twenty-one-year-old
civilian.* YOUNG FRANK *follows, tropical tan and uniform of
R.A.S.C. private.*)

YOUNG FRANK: It's so small.

IVOR: The houses look terrific small. I found that when I came
home.

YOUNG FRANK: But otherwise unchanged.

IVOR: *You've* changed. You've got a posh voice.

AMY: How scruffy he looked.

(IVOR *and* YOUNG FRANK *are embarrassed.* YOUNG FRANK
studies the collage.)

He still looks scruffy.

(AMY *goes off.*)

IVOR: Like a record? One of the old ones.

YOUNG FRANK (*as* IVOR *opens door revealing player*): The acoustic gramophone!

IVOR: Acoustic? Bloody hell. Used to be "wind-up".

YOUNG FRANK (*shrugs*): "Acoustic" is the proper word.

IVOR: Bloody hell. *Maple Leaf Rag*—or Beiderbecke's *Royal Garden*?

YOUNG FRANK: Tell the truth, Ivor, I find the insistent syncopation and predictable harmonies of jazz pretty boring these days.

IVOR (*imitation posh*): Oh, well, jolly good, what?

YOUNG FRANK: I've been listening a lot to Debussy and Ravel.

IVOR: Well, they were interested in jazz.

YOUNG FRANK: They transformed and elevated it.

FRANK: Poor prig.

(IVOR *shuts the door to the gramophone.*)

YOUNG FRANK: What's it like here?

IVOR: England? Bloody awful. Over in Germany you could get all the booze and fags you wanted, dead cheap. When I went first, you could get a Leica for a couple of bars of soap. Get a fräulein for a pound of coffee. And later on I had this bint, her parents were killed at Dresden. Couldn't half shag.

FRANK: The old familiar fear. Was I the only twenty-one-year-old virgin left?

IVOR: Worse than during the war here. Nothing in the shops, queues everywhere. Nobody cares that you've been doing your bit.

(AMY *comes in, wearing hat and coat.*)

AMY: Frank, I must run up to Montpelier's the bakers. Mrs. Stock says they've got some cream horns in. You still like cream horns?

YOUNG FRANK: Expect so. Can't remember.

AMY: If I hurry, there might be one or two left. What a business, queueing still! Ivor says there's plenty of everything in Germany. Well, it makes you wonder who won the war. (*Pause.*)

I blame the Labour Government.

YOUNG FRANK: Where I've spent the last three years, they aren't very upset about the shortage of cream horns.

AMY: Well, I don't suppose the Indians eat many cream horns. Even if they can get them. Mostly rice, isn't it?
(*Pause.* AMY *looks at* IVOR *for help. She continues.*)
I mean, they're not used to decent standards.

YOUNG FRANK: That's true, yes. I've sat in a Calcutta restaurant spending most of my pay on a tasty meal, with the faces of boys pressed against the window. Then the waiter sent them off and I saw them shoo the kitehawks from the dustbins and rummage through for anything the birds had left.

AMY: You must be glad to be home.

IVOR: Not our fault, though, is it?

AMY: Not our concern. We didn't send you out there, did we? And you didn't want to go. I said to Mrs. Bentley, well, it's silly, taking boys away from nice homes and sticking them down among a lot of natives.

FRANK: Thank Christ they did!

AMY: Exposing them to nasty diseases.

YOUNG FRANK: But—it *is* our concern. Your nice cup of tea comes from India, Mum. And your cotton dresses. The petrol for Dad's car and the tyres it runs on from the Middle East and Malaya. Most of the food he sells is grown in countries where people are starving: coffee, chocolate, cinnamon, pineapple, coconut, sugar, pepper . . . we rely on Asia and Africa for all that just as the posh people in London rely on Crewe for their Rolls-Royces.

IVOR: Hey, you sound like one of those blokes used to spout politics on the Downs.

AMY: Oh, them. Mother always pushed us children past. "Never mind them," she used to say, "we don't want our houses burnt down."

YOUNG FRANK: What did she mean by that?

IVOR: That's what politics leads to, isn't it?

AMY: I think there was a man saying he'd send people to burn our houses if we didn't vote for him.
(YOUNG FRANK *laughs. Pause.*)

IVOR: Politics are boring. Only thing is have a good time, like I did in Germany. Wine, women and song.

(YOUNG FRANK *goes up to look his last at the pin-up collage. He closes the door.* AMY *listens to* IVOR.)

Get a guitar . . . decent woman . . . one or two mates you can have a drink with . . . bit of money coming in but not too much . . . old car . . . paint some luminous dragons on it . . .

(YOUNG FRANK *looks at him and goes off.*)

. . . few Sidney Bechet records . . .

(*He takes out and lights a cigarette.*)

FRANK: Ivor tried to warm the embers for a few days but I went off to London to stay with one of my new service friends discussing E. M. Forster and personal relationships. Listening to Debussy.

(*They watch* IVOR *go off, smoking, after* YOUNG FRANK.)

AMY (*coming down*): He's never grown up, Ivor. Even now he's got six children, I call him Peter Pan.

FRANK: I wonder which of us retarded the other. He held back my understanding and I tried to spoil his good nature.

AMY: He was very good when Mother died, I've always had a soft spot for him because of that. Staying with her right to the end . . . banging the wardrobe to show there were no monkeys in it . . . telling her again and again there wouldn't be any more bombs.

(*Takes handkerchief from sleeve, blows nose.*)

Whenever some ordinary plane went over, she used to say, "Not those devils again?"

FRANK: I was watching a French film.

AMY: What?

FRANK: When she died.

AMY: Oh, you'd done a hard day's teaching, hadn't you, and in any case you were serious about films. What was it you wanted to be, when you were young?

FRANK: A director.

AMY: There you are. (*To Audience, as she goes.*) He's always ready to blame himself——

(*She goes.*)

FRANK: Gran was widowed in the First War, worked most of her

73

life in a factory and never had a penny to spare. When Ernest
Bevin was made Foreign Secretary, she was deeply shocked.
"He used to drive a mineral-water cart," she said, "and
wear a workman's cap; who's going to listen to *him*?"
(*Moves, thinks.*)
Who'd have thought I'd make a good teacher? Oh, at first
it was very much like the Schoolmaster Sketch.
(*Imitates Will Hay.*)
"Listen, will you answer my question—what is a unit of
electricity?" But my newly-developed sense of duty pre-
vailed and I began to think of myself as useful. My few
sexual encounters—the Domestic Science Teacher, for instance—finished painfully with everyone saying "sorry".
Then at a party I met Ursula again, the same brazen hussy
she'd always been but now twenty-three. She could spend
days on end in bed, smiling to show the pleasure she took,
mouthing obscenities when her tongue wasn't flicking in and
out of my ears and eyes and mouth. . . .
(*Recovers from the dream.*)
She never organized a thing in those days. But, of course,
what women hide is not their dark inner sexual core but
their urge to make arrangements. Still . . . laughing always
comes to crying, as my mother would say, and all this joy led
to a hasty scene at the register office. Our great coon of an
elder son gave Ursula such a kick in the stomach that at one
point she said "ow". And is that fifteen years ago? Nearly.
What's happened since? I took an external degree in the
evenings and joined the Social Studies Department of the
Technical College. Hands up who can guess where this
modern marvel is installed? In the evacuated orphanage.
After the grey crocodiles of under-privileged children, the
Air-Raid Wardens, the Black Americans, behold, the new
Men! . . . But I like it . . . I like them. Only somehow the
time since nineteen-fifty seems unconvincing and goes too
fast. The calendar pages fall away at silent film speed . . .
the forties are my golden age, my spiritual home The
Festival Hall, monument to ten years of austerity. I know
they were drab but austerity sounds so morally superior to

affluence, with its suggestions of sewage and greed and waste. What there was then was shared . . . people gave you lifts in their cars . . . and Ursula's father voted Labour in the hope this might continue. Well, these days he's got an enormous Vauxhall, a motor-mower, a Japanese cine-camera and holidays in the Black Forest, so——
(*Shrugs.*)
Whereas mine declined in fortune, retiring on a pension the size of which showed that other people had profited by his thrift. An enormous confidence-trick.
(*Moves upstage and opens door on radiogram. The living-room at home.*)
They couldn't afford repairs and Corinthian Villa began looking the worse for wear. The radio with the lightning-flash motif only cracked now, despite the old man's desperate struggles with its insides. The cube-shaped Staffordshire teapots had lost their lids. The only car in the avenue had passed to me and finally gone for scrap. Leonora, in which we'd driven on Sunday outings past the new factory estate —the concrete structures of Smith's Crisps, Crittall's Metal Windows and Top Dog Brake Linings. Whenever Ursula and I took the children to tea on Sunday, the house felt insufficient to contain those memories——
(*He pours himself a drink.* CHARLES *now comes in by another door, aged 75, wearing cardigan, shirt, flannels, slippers.*)
CHARLES: Where are you, Buzfuz?
(*They meet.*)
Look at this, boy. Just the job.
(*Holds out long pair of woollen underpants.*)
FRANK: Just the job for what?
CHARLES: I said to Mister Champness, the Big Cheese of men's outfitting, "These would be the very ticket for my son, whom you will remember as a mere boy but who has since become a huge ninny of nearly thirty, for ever complaining of the cold." I said, "Put me aside a dozen pairs."
FRANK: Are you still buying wholesale?
CHARLES: Cheaper by the dozen, boy.
FRANK: Only if you *want* a dozen.

75

CHARLES (*sharply*): D'you want them or not?

FRANK: Yes, thanks. If they're not too big.

CHARLES: Nothing worse than pants too small. Notice the gusset boy.

(*He handles it.*)

No restriction on your scrotum. Plenty of room for your parts. Easy access.

(*Sticks forefinger through the fly.*)

FRANK (*taking pants*): Right. Thanks very much.

CHARLES: Reminds me of my vicar turn. Did you ever hear my vicar turn, boy?

FRANK: Once or twice.

CHARLES (*mock-clerical*): And furthermore, dearly beloved brethren, let me scotch the rumour freely circulating in the parish that, if the curate wore his trousers the same way round as his collar, there wouldn't be nearly so many christenings to perform.

(*Returns to normal voice.*)

Bit smutty, boy? Used to go down well at the travellers' dinner.

(*Moves about, sniffs.*)

Smells like a four-ale bar in here.

FRANK: Mum told me to help myself to a drink.

CHARLES: Where *is* Old Mother Hubbard?

FRANK: Helping Ursula put Jenny to bed. I did Bill.

CHARLES: He's a fine boy, they're both fine children.

(FRANK *pours a drink.*)

If you'd seen the sights I saw as a youngster, you'd put strong liquor behind you. My old man—he was a master butcher—I've seen him so drunk he brought the cleaver down on his own hand. Standing there, his blood mingling with the blood of the lamb, swaying about shouting, "Bee-you-double gee-aye-arr the arr-you-double d-wye thing!" . . . and he wrapped a rag soaked in methylated spirits around his hand and finished hacking the joint . . . and when he lit a fag, boy, his fist was alight, enveloped in a bright blue flame. And he stood there laughing. Laughing, boy!

76

RANK: I fall asleep before I'm drunk and wake with a nasty head-
ache. It's not important any more. When people order a
pint these days, they more often mean milk.

CHARLES: I hear anyone pine for the Good Olde Days, I say, "For
goodness' sake hold your tongue, you can't possibly know
about what you're talking!" That frightens them to death,
boy——

RANK (*nodding*): Never put a preposition at——

CHARLES: That gets them groggy. Then I proceed to lay them
low with eloquent denunciation. Have you heard my epistle
to the Old Codgers on this question?

RANK: Yes.

CHARLES: You've missed a treat.

(*Sits, takes out and opens wallet. Takes from it a fat wad of
newspaper cuttings, many yellowed with age. He lays them
out carefully, sorting and separating.*)

And—as I happen to have a copy to hand——

(FRANK *looks at watch, drinks again. From a door comes* MISS
1940, *now dressed as a Hollywood slave girl, Tondelayo, all
bangles, briefs and long hair, she implores* FRANK *to help her.*
MR. MAGIC *follows, now a slave-trader with a whip. He threatens
the girl but* FRANK *with one kick sends him flying backwards
through the door.*)

Yes. This was the letter which riled me, written by some piecan from Ipswich. "Your article, the Dear Departed, stirred
in us many happy memories of the days of yesteryear. In
times like these, when the very air we breathe is full of
germs and atoms. . . .

(*The* SLAVE GIRL *embraces* FRANK'S *legs beseechingly. He
stands with his whisky looking down as she begins drawing
herself up his body, caressing him, circling him.*)

"When young layabouts wait at every corner, is it any
wonder old-age pensioners fear to walk abroad? But we
cherish fond thoughts of times when children honoured
their old folk, when a fair day's pay brought a fair day's
work" . . . you listening, crackpot?

(FRANK *was about to remove the* SLAVE GIRL'S *scanty clothing
but now he turns to* CHARLES *and she runs off.*)

77

FRANK: Yes.

CHARLES: "Cherish fond thoughts of times when children honoured their old folk, when a fair day's pay brought a fair day's work, sunny days when a farthing would buy untold dolly mixture." Which provoked from the Codgers the reply: "Not arf, Alfred. We reckon the likes of you and your missus can teach the rest of us a thing or two when it comes to the March of Time. Makes you wonder if we aren't all barmy!"

(Puts aside this cutting. Takes a piece of notepaper, much folded and worn.)

And here is my reply. "Oldster of Ipswich can hardly know about what he's talking. My memories are of a different ilk and may be summarized as the Three D's: dirt, drunkenness and disease. The twin stars of our tiny firmament were Big Jim, the fawning publican, and Ikey Stein the pawnbroker.

(Enter AMY and URSULA. AMY now 55 or so, neat and particular in twin-set and skirt, smoking a cigarette. URSULA is as at present, though may dress differently.)

On the streets women of ill-fame plied their unholy trade——

AMY: Oh, not this again! The Good Olde Days!

(She laughs and goes to drinks.)

CHARLES: Hold your tongue, Woodbine Winnie!

FRANK *(to URSULA)*: She gone down all right?

URSULA: She's playing with her plastic baa-lambs.

CHARLES: "Sitting here now before a cosy fire listening to the Eroica symphony of Beethoven, I am indeed——"

AMY: You like sherry, don't you, Ursula?

URSULA: Yes.

CHARLES: "I am indeed——"

FRANK: I'll get it.

CHARLES: "I am indeed——"

AMY: I'll have a vodka.

CHARLES: "I am indeed——"

AMY: Vodka and orange.

FRANK: All right.

CHARLES: Talking to myself here.

78

MY: Nobody asked you to.

(*Pause.* CHARLES *waits long-sufferingly.*)

CHARLES: "I am indeed happy to have heard the last of the Good Olde Days."

MY: I wish *we* had.

(*She sits.* URSULA *beside her.*)

CHARLES: "Yours Charles Bisley, Corinthian Villa, et cetera." Absolutely beyond my comprehension why they never printed it.

FRANK: Bit too *avant-garde* perhaps.

(*He is pouring drinks.* CHARLES *packs up cuttings.*)

CHARLES: Too what?

FRANK: I only mean it's a column *for* the simple-minded *by* the simple-minded. The most subversive they can get is oh, for the days when the poor knew their place and there was more sunshine. To which the only possible answer is most people were worse off and good riddance to pawnshops.

URSULA: Well, it's true!

FRANK: True but banal! These are the platitudes I was raised on!

CHARLES: On which I was——

FRANK: A pink map and a closed mind and believing what Lord Northcliffe's papers told you . . . and sitting there throughout the thirties being thankful you've got the only car in the avenue.

MY: Look out, Frank, you'll——

(*He pours too much orange into vodka and spills it.*)

URSULA: Too late!

FRANK: While Spain and the Rhineland and Abyssinia went on outside, not to mention the usual tyrannies in Africa and Asia.

MY: All over my clean carpet, oh dear.

URSULA: I'll get a cloth.

(*She goes.*)

FRANK (*putting orange on cabinet*): But God bless the Prince of Wales and shall we take the boy to Weymouth?

MY: If you'd stop talking for a second, Frank, you'd see that sticky orange is all over the carpet I've just shampooed.

CHARLES: Give him enough rope he'll hang himself.

79

FRANK: I'm trying to talk to you.

CHARLES: Talk? You talk? I will content myself with repeating to you what I said to Mister Lewthwaite of Fancy Goods.

(URSULA *returns with floorcloth and* AMY *rubs the floor*.)

AMY: Thanks, Ursula, I'll do it.

CHARLES: You remember him, Buzfuz? Little squirt of a fellow, about so high, pronounced stammer. I kept trying to get a word in edgewise but he was bah-bah-bahing away. I said, "Mister Lewthwaite, I haven't got all day to stand here listening to your speech impediment." And I added, "Leave the talking to those with a gift of the gab. And—at the risk of blowing my own trumpet . . . for, after all——"

(*Mock clerical*.) "Verily, verily, I say unto you, blessed is he that bloweth his own trumpet, lest it be not blown at all."

(URSULA *is laughing and he is playing to her.* FRANK *has swallowed a drink and has opened a door to find the scantily-clad* SLAVE GIRL *bound by her wrists, struggling to free herself. As she sees him, she cowers back in terror*.)

You should have seen his face, Ursula. I said, "When it comes to talking none is more able"—notice, Buzfuz, none *is* more able, not none *are*—— .

(FRANK *comes back, shutting the door, impatiently listening t* CHARLES.)

"none is more able than the weird, wise and wonderful Colossus, Charles the First and Foremost." I said, "Good day to you, friend," and left him gasping, boy, thinking to himself——

AMY: Good riddance to bad rubbish——

CHARLES: "Good riddance to b——" —what d'you mean, good riddance? Hold your tongue, Capstan Connie. No, I left him thinking, "That man is a veritable marvel. How was he born so wonderful?——"

AMY: Why was he born at all?

CHARLES: "Why was he born——"

(*Breaks off again.* URSULA *is laughing.* FRANK *is staring with a stone face.* CHARLES *looks at him.* AMY *has done the carpet and sits again, drinking*.)

Never one to outstay my welcome, Ursula, I shall leave yo

to your own devices for a moment while I use the convenience.

(*He goes.*)

AMY: I believe he's worse the older he gets.

URSULA: No, he's lovely.

FRANK: All very well for you to come and find him amusing
now, now he's become a comedian.

(*Gives her her sherry, women sit drinking,* CHARLES *reappears
at same door.*)

CHARLES: Talking about the old man the moment his back's
turned?

(*Comes in.*)

No, I meant to say apropos of the Good Olde Days——

AMY: You set my teeth on edge about the Good Olde Days.

CHARLES: —think of your own enviable position, the advantages
you had. Look at your lovely house, central heating—not
that I like it, dries your mouth, I find, but very nice if
you're used to it. No central heating here, that's because I
gave up so much to give you a good education.

FRANK: Good education!

CHARLES: Fed and clothed you, gave you everything a boy could
want, threw my money about——

AMY: Like a Jew with no arms——

CHARLES: Like a Jew with no arms. Who said that? Goldflake
Gertie again? I'll give you a kick in the pants.

AMY: Why don't you go on up to the toilet?

CHARLES: And look at you, with a university degree, a wonderful
job, teaching grown-up people, imparting your knowledge.
Superannuation scheme.

(FRANK *howls with derision.*)

Nothing to laugh at. I made sure of my pension.

AMY: Lot of good it's done us, too. Navvies earn more than us
these days.

FRANK: Don't you think they should?

CHARLES: You should be grateful, boy.

URSULA: He is.

CHARLES: Just as I'm proud, Ursula. Proud to have helped my son
up the ladder a few steps. If I've done that and it's appreci-

F   81

ated, my life will not have been in vain.

(*Takes out handkerchief.* URSULA *looks at* FRANK *as though demanding that he express some thanks. He doesn't.*)

Oh, I've made mistakes in my time, I admit it. In a life as full as the Old Man's, it would have been a miracle not to have made the odd mistake. Perhaps some I shall regret until the day I pass away.

(*Pause.* URSULA *looks at him.* AMY *drinks.*)

(*Suddenly.*) This shirt was a mistake!

(*Pulls out his shirt-tail.*)

I like a shirt I can wrap round my buttocks and keep me warm. I said to Mister Champness, "Next time give me a shirt big enough for Lockhart's."

URSULA: Lockhart's?

AMY: What's he on about now?

URSULA: Private parts.

CHARLES: What?

URSULA: Rhyming slang!

CHARLES: No! Big enough for Lockhart's Elephants. They were the great music-hall turn when I was a nipper. Nothing to do with private parts, young woman. What d'you think of her, Amy? Got a one-track mind, I should think.

AMY: Your endless chatter makes my head sing, I know that.

CHARLES: No wonder she's got two nippers already. I shouldn't let young crackpot make so free with you in the jolly old double-bed.

AMY: Very nice. Could we change the subject?

CHARLES: Not having another, are you?

URSULA: Not yet.

CHARLES: I only thought when I saw you this afternoon, by Jove, Ursula's breasts look swollen.

AMY: Take no notice, dear, I don't.

CHARLES: She never takes a scrap of notice of me, Old Mother Hubbard. Do you?

(*Goes down on one knee by her and tries to kiss her. She recoils.*)

AMY: Not a scrap. Why don't you go to the toilet?

CHARLES: No chance of a spot of slap-and-tickle these days.

82

URSULA (*moving to* FRANK, *they stand watching*): See what I mean about touching?

FRANK: I know all about that.

URSULA: Kiss him, you block of ice! More bothered with your shampooed carpet than your man.

(CHARLES *stands*.)

CHARLES: I sometimes think of the chances I missed, the girls I turned away. Vicky Edmunds, for instance, lived in Leytonstone. I wonder what Vicky's doing now.

AMY: Drawing the old age pension, I should think.

CHARLES: Drawing the old age——?

(*Goes to door, turns.*)

I shall boil a kettle to fill my hot-water bottle. Once in bed, I shall place it scalding between my thighs.

AMY: I don't think Ursula's interested in what you do in bed.

CHARLES: Nobody is these days. Which accounts for the waterbottle. A last resort, eh, Ursula?

(URSULA *stops him on his way out, kisses him. He goes on out.*)

AMY: D'you think he's gone for good? Are we going to enjoy a conversation for a change?

(URSULA *looks at* FRANK *but he has turned away. She goes to stand near* AMY.)

No, what I was saying upstairs was we could have the children for a day or two so you and Frank could go away.

URSULA: D'you think it's possible?

AMY: Frank could do with a break, he looks so drawn.

URSULA: Would Mister Bisley mind?

AMY: Him? No. He'll take Bill to the park, give him something to occupy his mind, instead of hanging about the house and getting in my way. He's under my feet the whole day long otherwise.

(*Door opens near* FRANK *and* MR. MAGIC *throws the* SLAVE GIRL *to the ground at* FRANK's *feet.* MR. MAGIC *now seems to be a eunuch and threatens the* SLAVE GIRL *with a whip. He bows to* FRANK. FRANK *raises her from the ground and stands her before him. There is no pause in* AMY's *speech.*)

Tell the truth, he hasn't known what to do since retirement.

URSULA: I thought he enjoyed it.

AMY: After his fashion, yes, pottering about, getting in my way.

URSULA: He's got so many interests. Music, rugby, cricket——

AMY: When he was on the road, at least he was out from under my feet from Monday to Friday.

(FRANK *reaches out and tears the brassière off the* SLAVE GIRL. *She flinches and turns her head away.* FRANK *stares at her.*)

But now he won't go anywhere, he sits listening to his blessed records. I give him something to do now and then, nothing difficult. Well, he's like a baby half the time, he knocked a pot of plastic emulsion down the stairs last May. And only yesterday he vacuumed an enormous leaf off the rubber-plant in the greenhouse.

(FRANK *gestures to* MR. MAGIC, *who turns* SLAVE GIRL *so that she submits to* FRANK, *raising one leg. He takes her ankle in his hands and begins to remove her bangles.*)

And sometimes I think if I don't get out of the house, I shall go stark, staring mad.

URSULA: Perhaps after all those years travelling, he wants to settle down.

AMY: Settle down? Fossilize! I feel like a fossil in a glass case.

(*Seems on the edge of an emotional outburst but* URSULA *stares at her unsympathetically so* AMY *blows nose in handkerchief and turns to* FRANK.)

Frank!

(*He goes on taking off the* SLAVE GIRL'S *bangles.*)

Look at him, dreaming again. Always got his head in the clouds. Frank!

FRANK: Hullo?

(*Turns from* SLAVE GIRL *She and* MR. MAGIC *go out through nearest door.* FRANK *comes to* AMY *and* URSULA.)

AMY: I was telling Ursula, Dad vacuumed a leaf off the rubber-plant yesterday.

FRANK (*absently*): Oh, dear.

AMY: Yes. I found him trying to put it back with a tube of Evo-Stik. You do look drawn, don't you think so, Ursula? Working too hard at college? Reading too much? I think you can overdo reading.

84

(FRANK *leans over* URSULA *and kisses her. She recoils.*
CHARLES *reappears wearing white overall and yachting cap,
carrying broom in one hand and flat twelve-inch square box
in other.*)

CHARLES: He's back and to prove it he's here!

AMY: Thought that was too good to last.

CHARLES: Well, boy, what d'you think?

FRANK: What?

CHARLES: The turn-out. Do I look the part?

FRANK: Depends what the part is. If it's Camille, for instance,
no, you don't.

CHARLES: They've been appealing in the local press for volunteer
Lollipop Men to patrol the crossings at the council school.
Old Mother Hubbard drew my attention, saying it might
get me out from under her feet for an hour a day, so I went
to the police station for particulars. D'you know what the
constable said, boy? "You better wait till the sergeant gets
back." He was only a nipper with a brand-new uniform. I
thought, "Hullo, this is just up my street." I said, "Oh?"
very slowly, you know, Ursula, that gets them groggy——

FRANK (*desperately*): Oh, God!

CHARLES: I said, "Well, Officer," always call them "officer",
makes them look very small, "Well, Officer, will you tell
your sergeant that due to your indifference, he has lost his
only opportunity of a Lollipop Man *par excellence*! And
next time—not so much of the jolly old buck. Good morning." I walked off and left him gasping.

AMY: Left him wondering if you'd escaped from Dr. Fox's.

CHARLES: I'm never one to creep or crawl to people, Ursula,
you've noticed that? High on my list of dislikes: creepers,
what-I-call Masonic types. Those who climb by licking aye-
ar-ess-ee-ess. Little Lofty Lewthwaite sucking up to Mister
Tombs. Some years ago I learned the oaths of allegiance
with the sole purpose of baiting my colleagues in the Lodge.
Friend Lewthwaite said to me, "Freemasonry is Bah-Bah-
Bah-Bah-Brotherly Love." I said, "It's all my eye and Bah-
bah-Betty Martin." Now among his disabilities is a pronounced cast in one eye and whenever he's getting flum-

moxed, this eye starts swivelling round, you know, as though he's looking for an avenue of escape. My Number One Anathema: Creepers. Have you heard my list of dislikes?

FRANK ⎫
AMY ⎭ Yes.

CHARLES: I was asking your good lady here.

URSULA (*laughing*): I don't know.

FRANK (*to her*): We had it last time we came here!

CHARLES (*to* URSULA): You've missed a treat. (*To* FRANK.) Put this away, boy.

(FRANK *angrily leans broom on back wall.* CHARLES *begins listing on his fingers.*)

Creepers. Filth in all forms: filthy finger-nails, filthy talk, dog's soil on the footpath. I put up a sign on the tree outside: "Dog-owners:

Let it not be said unto your shame

That all was beauty here until you came."

AMY: And I took it down again.

CHARLES: And cork-tipped Katey took it down again.

AMY: Don't want the neighbours reading that.

CHARLES: Where was I, Ursula?

AMY: Think we've escaped from Dr. Fox's.

URSULA: Filth in all its forms.

CHARLES: Bartok. Unmelodious, I always think. The scent of hyacinths, which invariably brings back the cemeteries of childhood. People who talk about the Good Olde Days. Spitting. Beards and long hair. Unsightly. (*Touches hair at* FRANK'*s neck.*) The Principal of your college looks at you and thinks: "Young Bisley, not a bad lecturer, speaks out clearly like a sergeant-major, gets that from his father, but his hair looks poverty-stricken." I've been in business all my life, I know about what I'm talking.

(*Lists again on fingers.* FRANK *moves upstage.*)

Booze. Creepers.

URSULA: Masonic types.

CHARLES: You've got it, gal.

URSULA: We've had those.

(CHARLES *moves after* FRANK *and confers with him quietly, showing the flat box.*)

AMY: Mister Lewthwaite sponsored Charles for his lodge but nothing came of it. Well, I don't think they wanted to have to promote him off the road and into the wholesale depot. They none of them liked him. I was quite relieved, of course, it meant he was out from under my feet Monday to Friday, though it would have meant a better salary and pension.
(FRANK *looks at contents of box: long-playing records.*
CHARLES *comes down again, leaving* FRANK *to put on record.*
CHARLES *brings a leaflet in his hand.*)

CHARLES: And then, of course, my list of likes.

AMY: Likes and dislikes, good old days, you'll have us all in Dr. Fox's.

CHARLES: Pay no heed to the O.M.H. (*Lists again.*) Cleanliness of thought and body. Giving people a fair chance in life. A fair day's work for a fair day's pay. Sometimes I sit in the front-room armchair watching the municipal highway cleaners standing about. I said to one of them, "Mind you don't have an accident, friend, and fall off your broom." Next: the ideals of the Co-operative Movement. A roaring fire. (*Considers.*) On reflection, I'm not sure I wouldn't put a roaring fire *before* the ideals of the Co-operative Movement. Comfortable chairs. Not those nasty things you've got, Ursula.

URSULA: Thanks very much.

AMY: Don't take any notice. He doesn't know. (*To* CHARLES.) They're functional. Ursula's got everything functional.

CHARLES: It may be *functional* as Old Harry, but I can't *sit* in it! I keep on slipping *down*.
(*Music begins.* FRANK *has put on a record. Grieg's* Hall of The Mountain King. CHARLES *begins dancing and conducting.*)

URSULA: Oh, good. I was just about to ask for music.

AMY: Bang-bang-bang-bang.

CHARLES: You're a music-lover, Ursula?

URSULA: There was never any in our house but I'm——

CHARLES: I played this once to Lofty Lewthwaite on the old seventy-eights. I said, "This is Grieg's immortal music for the

87

well-known play *Peer Gynt*." I said, "You've heard about
Henrik Ibsen, haven't you?" He had his hand cupped over
his ear, he's a bit on the deaf side, Ursula. I shouted, "Henrik
Ibsen!" "Oh, yes," he said, "I knew him well. Dah-dah-
drapery manager at Exeter branch." I said, "Who's that?"
He said, "Hah-hah-Henry Gibson." Well, I roared, Ursula, I
couldn't help it, perhaps I shouldn't have, he was an in-
fluential man, chief buyer in Fancy Goods. I said, "Not
Henry Gibson, friend. Henrik Ibsen came from nah-nah-
Norway." He didn't like it, you know.

AMY: I shouldn't think he did.

CHARLES: I never creep and crawl. I won't.

(*Reads from leaflet, conducting the record.*)

"Hearthstone Concert Hall. Sixty-five complete selections of
light classical music by thirty-eight immortal composers.
These are the tunes to set toes tapping, heads nodding,
fingers drumming" . . . or in Mister Lewthwaite's case, eyes
swivelling, eh, boy?

(URSULA *laughs.* FRANK *is looking through the other records.*)

"For Father, the hard-pressed business man, a musical education without tears. For Mother, almost twelve hours of
companionship to keep the blues at bay. To help you waltz
through the dish-washing."

AMY: I don't think. Bang-bang-bang-bang, all day long.

URSULA: I thought you liked music.

AMY: In its proper place.

(URSULA *appeals to* FRANK, *who comes down to join them.*)

CHARLES: And listen to this, Old Mother Hubbard, listen, here's
the bit you'll like: "At Almost Half the Price in the Shops.
Music your family will bless you for." (*He tut-tuts dis-
approvingly.*) Music for which your family will——

AMY: Just a minute.

CHARLES: "Costs absolutely nothing."

AMY: Is this something you've bought?

(*Goes to him. He moves away.*)

This music? Is it one of these records? Is it?

CHARLES (*laughing*): No, wait a minute, Amy. "Costs nothing to
receive this astounding bargain——"

AMY: Oh, yes, I'll bet. But something to keep it.

CHARLES: No, wait a minute. Come and help me, boy.

(*She chases him about as he holds the leaflet out of her reach.*)

CHARLES (*reading*): "Handel's *Largo*, one of the all-time greats of music!"

(*She runs at him again but he dodges her and moves across with the leaflet, laughing.*)

Butterfingers, butterfingers. You'll have to move more smartly than that to get the better of the old man.

(AMY *bursts into tears. Everyone astonished and upset.*)

FRANK: Give it to her.

(*Takes leaflet from* CHARLES *and gives it to* AMY, *who reads it, sobbing aloud.* FRANK *comes down.*)

(*To Audience.*) I'm trying to remember exactly how sad it was. But in retrospect it seems funny.

AMY: Fifteen pounds! It costs fifteen pounds. Then you can send it back.

CHARLES (*subdued*): I can't do that, Amy.

AMY: You've had it on approval, you can say you don't like it.

CHARLES: I've sent the cheque off.

AMY: I don't believe it.

CHARLES: Wonderful bargain. Fifteen pounds——

AMY: He does it to spite me.

(*Cries even more.* CHARLES *hasn't managed the moment as he planned and doesn't know what to do.* FRANK *takes off the record.* URSULA *stands near* CHARLES. AMY *recovers and speaks to the Audience.*)

Only last week I asked for the money for a new spring outfit and he said we couldn't run to it. As though he hasn't got enough blasted records banging away all day and night.

FRANK: Why don't you take some interest in his music? Isn't that one of your common interests?

CHARLES: You hold your tongue, Sonny Jim.

FRANK: Sonny Jim? I'm nearly forty. A middle-aged man with three whopping kids.

URSULA: No, at this time you were nearly thirty and Matthew hadn't been born.

FRANK: Oh, Christ!

CHARLES: Don't take the Lord's name in vain.

FRANK: The Lord's name? You haven't been inside a church since my christening. The nearest you've come to godliness is cleanliness.

AMY: You've no idea what I have to go through with him, week in, week out.

FRANK: But you're to blame as well.

AMY (*frightened*): Me? To blame?

FRANK: You make no effort to understand him.

AMY: I don't expect much. No car, we never go on holiday, the house is falling about our ears. Talks of mending things, he potters about, you ought to see him wall-papering, talk about butterfingers then! I'm only saying I expect a certain standard. Don't you think at our age you deserve a certain standard? Ursula? Don't you?

URSULA: I've never taken any standard for granted. It has to be worked for. Marriage has to be worked *at*. Understanding has to be achieved by hard work.

FRANK: Let it go.

URSULA: No, why should we allow them to use us as shock-absorbers? Every time they postpone their fights until we visit them. It's easy to blame your father but she's worse.

CHARLES: Now don't you raise your voice against Mrs. Bisley.

FRANK (*to* URSULA): There!

AMY: He's getting round me now. Like when he buys another lot of junk. Twelve straw boaters he brought home last week.

CHARLES: A dozen for half-a-sovereign, Amy. That's less than a shilling each.

AMY: Oh, wonderful, if you happen to know twelve people who want straw boaters.

CHARLES: Say young crackpot here wants to do a Nigger Minstrel turn at his college show——

FRANK (*to Audience*): But with his late-Victorian, Edwardian background—'Appy 'Ampstead, Derby Day, drunk for twopence and women were either old maids or always pregnant——

AMY: Our family wasn't like that, thank you——

90

FRANK (*continuing*): —his way out was to resist the indulgences that gave pleasure to the poor—drink, tobacco, gambling, lechery, language. The harmless sedatives that, taken in small doses, might have made branch managers and other travellers welcome him instead of turning away.

CHARLES (*to Audience, too*): Nobody ever turned away from the old man——

FRANK: I went with you. I saw them dodging out through the back doors. You were an embarrassment, you were dreaded. That clothing factory where you got me fitted for wholesale suits, with that man whose every other word was bloody and who used to wink at me while you tut-tutted and kept on going bee-ell-double-o——

CHARLES: I had occasion to reprimand him several——

FRANK: Then the walk back through the factory with all those girls at their machines whistling at me and shouting, "What are you doing tonight, dearie?"—to which the only truthful answer would have been, "Wetting the bed."

CHARLES: I didn't realize it upset you, boy. They were only common girls.

FRANK (*to* AMY): I'm trying to make the point that his nature demanded some addiction, some indulgence. And his occupation showed the way: bargains, something for nothing.

CHARLES: We're getting a lecture, now, Amy.

FRANK: I suppose this is *my* occupational hazard. Lecturing.

CHARLES: We're not your students.

URSULA: It might not hurt you to listen, though.

CHARLES: Oh, d'you hear that, fag-end Fanny? We can profit from piecan's education here.

AMY: If you call me that once again, I shall scream. An occasional cigarette's not much to ask. In our family we were poor but happy. Mother was widowed twice but she brought us up, my brother and I. She slaved in a factory.

CHARLES (*conciliatory*): She was a dear old soul.

AMY: She enjoyed a drink, a laugh and a song. When I told her we were marrying, she said, "Considering you could have had your pick, you chose a miserable devil."

URSULA: Why did you marry him then?

AMY: I didn't know any better. I was only a girl.

CHARLES: Twenty-eight.

AMY: What about you? Middle-aged *you* were.

CHARLES: Yes.

AMY: And set in your ways, like a fossil.

CHARLES: And I was her Last Chance, Ursula. Last Chance
  Charlie, eh, boy? Saved her bacon.

AMY: I had plenty of chances, then and later on. I only didn't
  take them for the boy's sake.

FRANK: That's enough, Mum.

AMY: He knows very well.

  (CHARLES *moves upstage and packs up his box of records.*)
  Because, after a time, it's not just what you want to do, is
  it? No, after a time, only the children count. And though
  Frank used to say sometimes, while he was away, "Let's
  go off somewhere——"

FRANK: No!

AMY: Oh, yes, (*back to Audience*) but I wanted him to finish his
  schooling and how could I have been sure with anyone
  else——?

FRANK: Will you shut up!

  (CHARLES *goes off, taking record and broom, without turning
  back.*)

AMY: You did say, that, Frank.

FRANK: I didn't understand him then.

AMY: Oh, I don't *understand* him even now.

FRANK: Well. Perhaps Ursula's helped me.

AMY (*to Audience*): Easy for her. So late in the day.
  (*Goes off.*)

FRANK: We only seem to understand people when there's no
  longer any need. When that phase of our life is over.

URSULA: You mean we understand each other.

FRANK: What?

URSULA: Well, you've left me, we're living apart. That phase is
  over.

  (FRANK *takes this in. Then to Audience.*)

FRANK: The day finished at eight o'clock, all tense and awkward
  trying to pretend nothing had happened.

92

URSULA: We carried the sleeping children down to the car and made subdued farewells at the gate.

FRANK: Dad told me for the billionth time how to point the car in the right direction. "I should go down the avenue, along Appian Terrace and up Tuscan Vale to the main road——"

URSULA: As soon as they were out of sight, I felt sorry for them both.

FRANK: And excited.

URSULA: What?

FRANK: We were excited. After we'd put the kids to bed, you went for a bath and I came in and had you, all warm and slippery, my belly slapping the surface of the water——
(*She makes for the door and goes out as soon as he starts on this subject. He runs to the slammed door, opens it and shouts after her.*)
—I made you groan, deep down in your throat! Your tongue was everywhere, like before we were married!
(*Shuts door, moves back.*)
Control yourself, man. Have you finished packing?
(*Looks into open suitcase.*)
Put in some sexy deodorant, case some lady lecturer or nymphet student spots your potentialities?
(*Holds up after-shave.*)
Yes.
(*Dreams again.*)
After retirement, the old man gave up packing. Hardly ever left Corinthian Villa. So, to save Mum from fossilizing, we took her to a film from time to time. Or she would baby-sit if we were invited out. I'd drive over to fetch her and, while she put her coat on, Dad would give me one of his comic turns.
(FRANK *imitates* CHARLES.)
You've heard my lists of likes, boy? I should think so. I've got something to add thereto. A brush for doing your back! There always seems to be an area right in the small of the back I just can't reach with a nail-brush. So look here . . .
(*Mimes bringing brush from behind back.*) A lovely old-fashioned job with a long handle. (*Himself.*) Very good.

93

CHARLES: Found it on someone's dustbin.

(AMY *has come on, wearing outdoor coat, hat, etc.*)

Only don't tell Old Mother Hubbard.

AMY: Someone's dustbin! You said you bought it in a sale.

FRANK (*as* CHARLES): Now look where you've got me, Frank, you great crackpot. Right into hot water.

AMY: You never know what kind of people have been using it before us. You get rid of it, do you hear?

FRANK (*as* CHARLES): Keep your hair on, O.M.H. You ready?

AMY: Have I kept you waiting, Frank? (*She puts on gloves.*)

FRANK (*as* CHARLES): Have you got everything? Mintoes? Spectacles?

AMY: Yes.

FRANK (*as* CHARLES): Laxatives?

AMY: We're going to the theatre.

FRANK (*himself*): He led us out to the pavement, laughing and excited, picked up a passing child and stood him on our front wall. Then turned on the child's father and told him to take his hands from his pockets and stand up straight.

AMY: Wasn't that awful? A man of thirty-five.

FRANK (*as* CHARLES): Which way you going, Frank? Down the avenue, perhaps, along Appian Terrace and up Tuscan Vale to——

AMY: D'you think Frank doesn't know the way by this time?

FRANK (*himself*): I shot the car away from the kerb as he belatedly signalled that the way was clear. In the nearside wing-mirror, I saw him picking rubbish from the gutter.

AMY: Fancy a dirty old brush from someone's dustbin!

FRANK: When I brought you home afterwards, the "Eine Kleine Nachtmusik" was being played so loud we couldn't make him hear the doorbell.

AMY: I didn't want to get my key out but in the end I had to.

FRANK: He was lying dead on the kitchen floor, his milk boiling over.

AMY: He must have gone very suddenly. The best way.

FRANK: Oh, yes.

AMY: Funny thing, a few days earlier he'd asked for a drop of Scotch, where before he wouldn't even eat a trifle if he

94

detected sherry.

FRANK: I always seem to be in cinemas or theatres while my relatives are dying.

AMY: Not your fault, though, is it?

FRANK: D'you realize, while he was lying there with the milk and Mozart, we were in the same theatre where one night during the war—d'you remember, Mum?

AMY: What?

(*Music. Lights change.* MR. MAGIC *comes on as comedian, wearing mock elegant outfit and removes gloves in parody of toff.* MISS 1940 *comes on as a showgirl and takes them for him. He also removes hat and overcoat and she takes these, grinning, swinging hips. As she goes off, passing him, he pinches her and she gives shocked squeak and smile. He looks after her. Then turns to Audience.*)

MR. MAGIC: No use you looking. That's under the counter, that is. But I'll tell you this for nothing: she's got a beautiful little chihuahua. She has. Very fond of it, too. She showed her friend and her friend said: "Yes, lovely, but those little short hairs aren't right. You want to get rid of those." So she went to the chemist, she said, "I want something to get rid of little short hairs." He gave her some ointment, he said, "Rub it on your legs twice a day." See? She said, "It's not for me legs." He said, "No?" She said, "No, it's for me little chihuahua." He said, "In that case don't ride your bike for a fortnight." No—listen! A little monologue. There was an old cow from Huddersfield——

(*From auditorium comes a single slow handclap. Comedian pauses.*)

CHARLES (*from Audience*): Get off!

AMY: Yes, I remember this.

CHARLES: Women and children present. If you can't do better than that, get off!

(*Continues slow clap.*)

MR. MAGIC: Now don't you knock your pipe out at me, Grandpa. You don't know how lucky you are. This is all continental stuff I'm giving you.

CHARLES: No more filth! Get off home!

FRANK: I sat there, hot under the collar of my utility shirt.

MR. MAGIC: I'll tell you what. We'll put it to the vote.

FRANK: I've hated audience participation ever since.

AMY: I tried to shut him up.

CHARLES: Get off! No more smut.

(*He has come down the aisle and is standing by the stage, still giving the handclap. From other parts of audience come boos and cries of "Shut up" and "Throw him out".*)

(*To Audience.*) Don't talk so big, you make yourself look small.

MR. MAGIC: No, give him a chance——

CHARLES (*coming on to stage*): Anyone who has to resort to the private parts of women to get a laugh——

(*Cries of "Shame".*)

AMY: Come on home, Charles. Everyone's looking.

CHARLES: Many of us have our wives and children with us here tonight.

FRANK: Yet I was proud of him.

MR. MAGIC: Now, listen, Dad, I only mentioned a chihuahua.

CHARLES: Cleanliness is next to godliness.

MR. MAGIC: All right, mate, I've nearly finished anyway. (*To Audience.*) I'll come back in the second half after he's gone.

(*Goes off, to cheers.* CHARLES *remains with* FRANK *and* AMY.)

CHARLES: Jokes about conveniences and bee-you-double-gee-ee-are-why.

(*Loud boos.* CHARLES *turns in their direction and bows, slowly, with dignity.*)

I bowed slowly, boy, you remember?

FRANK: Shall I ever forget?

CHARLES: Frightened the life out of them.

AMY: You don't care how much you embarrassed me, I could hear people saying, "He's escaped from Dr. Fox's."

CHARLES: For a moment I toyed with the idea of giving an excerpt from my most successful recitation "Jeremiah in the Turkish bath".

(*Takes posture and recites in Cockney dialect.*)

"And now, Jerry, if you'll lie on the table here, I'll just finish you awf."

FRANK: All right, Dad, thanks——

CHARLES (*after extravagant horrified reaction*): "Finish me awf?"

FRANK: Yes, fine, that's enough now.

(*They try to usher him towards a door. He escapes, returns front.*)

CHARLES: "I'm darned near finished awf already."

FRANK: Come on, you've had your turn.

AMY (*to Audience, while* MEN *argue in whispers*): The band struck up and the dancing girls came on and he ran down the aisle peering at them through his opera glasses, cheering.

CHARLES (*to her*): Nothing smutty about the female form. Only lewd innuendo.

FRANK: Right. Thank you.

AMY (*persuading him through the door again*): Soon after that I got him into the foyer and on to the bus.

(*Shuts door.*)

FRANK (*to Audience*): Well, the day of the funeral——

(*Door reopens.* CHARLES *again.*)

CHARLES (*continuing recitation*): "I've been pushed and pum-melled, pummelled and pushed. I'm black and blue."

FRANK: Will you let me tell the rest of the story!

CHARLES: You tell a story, boy? You couldn't make a pudden crawl!

FRANK: And you're dead! So go!

(*Cheers from Audience.* CHARLES *looks at* FRANK, *then at Audience, bows slowly three times to mounting derision, then goes, leaving door open.* FRANK *runs to it, slams it, waits, then returns to front.*)

The day of the funeral a heatwave started. The streets had long ago been turned into car-parks by students of my tech., the orphanage opposite. So, where once had stood the only car in the avenue, there was now barely room to squeeze his hearse in.

AMY: Mister Lewthwaite turned up at the crematorium. And Mister Champness, of men's outfitting.

FRANK: "Man that is born of woman hath but a short time to live and is full of misery. He cometh up and is cut down like a flower," said the priest, and pressed a button and the coffin sank. I remember wondering if they'd taken off Dad's ankle bandages.

AMY: Oh, I should think so.

FRANK: And when it had sunk far enough, a blue cover slid across. Was it the minister or someone below operating all these gadgets?

AMY: He was a good man, your father. A good husband. I could have done much worse. He never kept me short. He had his funny ways, it's true, but who hasn't?

FRANK: After that we had to clear his rubbish——

AMY: Oh, that was one of his funny ways. Hoarding. Two great attics and a garage full of junk.

FRANK: But the garage wasn't large enough to contain the mounting collection and it spilt into the back garden, filling the rusty Morrison shelter. Framed group photographs of the grocery travellers, with Dad solemn and forward-looking. Sacks of solidified cement.

AMY: Four gas-masks in their cases. One was Mother's.

FRANK: My army uniform. Boxes of golf-balls.

AMY: All that ointment in the medicine chest.

FRANK: Once in the loft, when I was a boy, I'd found two golden sovereigns along with some cast-off teeth. But now there was only trash. I opened a promising brown paper parcel to find an empty suitcase.

AMY: I think you enjoyed it, though. Ursula came and helped shampoo the carpets. It was nice to see the place looking nice.

FRANK: There was the window-display for hair-cream. A thirties man with George Raft hair and an arm brushing it that moved to and fro by an electro-magnet.

AMY: Fancy keeping that.

FRANK: One or two old photographs. Dad's mother frowning from a grainy scene beside a horse and cart——

AMY: All in black, with her hair strained back and her lips a thin white line. Don't tell me. No wonder his father drank. I remember the first time she saw you, in her home, straight out of Dickens. I was trying to bath you, Frank, in a tub on the table with the gaslight low to save money. She stood there criticizing: "You should wear glasses," she said, when I nearly let you slip. "Stop thinking about your looks and get some glasses." I finished up in tears, which is what she wanted. And I thought to myself, "What have I come into?" In our family we were poor but happy. Mother enjoyed a drink, a laugh and a song.

(*Turns and goes, closing door.*)

FRANK: His death made me feel the likelihood, the certainty, of my own. I was the oldest man in the family now. The greater part of my life was behind me. Teach us to number our days that we may apply our hearts unto wisdom. Wisdom. Not the messy obstacle-race that starts with the first child's cry of "Not fair" and ends at night with man and wife facing each other like exhausted wrestlers . . . trying to remember what we meant to say to each other earlier on when we couldn't make ourselves heard. Usually I'd postpone sleep with the only entertainment I could offer in bed—an indecent assault with Ursula yawning like a dog in my face. So, as I said, one day, I had the long-awaited brainstorm. The brainstorm the old man never reached. Once you decide to go, you'd be surprised how easy it is. We cling to our pain out of habit and the fear of worse. I'm glad to have admitted at last there was no need to share her domestic insanities simply because we'd slept together and enjoyed each other. That wasn't applying our hearts unto wisdom. But, I may not be able to stay away for ever. Dependence dies hard and anyway there's the money. The flat's cheap, I live frugally . . . which is a pleasure after the plastic and paper filth of the scene at home. And I sometimes bring young women here for private tutorials. Play Eddie Condon records. Slightly grizzled, quizzical middle-aged bit. You know—seen it all. Silver pubes among the gold. I don't mean nastiness. On the contrary—tender episodes between consenting adults. And why not? Somewhere between the black-out and the marriage-bed I missed young love, ecstasy, surrender. I suddenly saw my elder son approaching the age when he'd claim the benefits of the new state I'd helped to bring about . . . and it was so unfair!

(YOUNG FRANK *comes on, aged fourteen again, but dressed as modern adolescent, with suitable hair.*)

Hullo, Bill.

YOUNG FRANK: You alone?

FRANK: As usual.

(YOUNG FRANK *nods, moves about,* FRANK *watches him.*)

Your mother sent you?

YOUNG FRANK: She wouldn't.

FRANK (*nodding*): No.

YOUNG FRANK: She doesn't wish to know about you.

FRANK: Just passing, eh?

YOUNG FRANK: Kind-of.

FRANK: On that motor-bike? Was that you on that motor-bike making such a filthy row revving all up the street?

YOUNG FRANK: It's Tom's, yeah.

FRANK: Well, I'm sure I can speak for the whole street when I say it was tremendously impressive. I'm sure even the people who'd managed to get to sleep before you arrived were tremendously impressed when you woke them up.

(YOUNG FRANK *finds* FRANK'*s records and looks at the sleeves.*)

Still, perhaps Tom could keep it quieter when you go be-cause those poor sleepless wage-slaves might have to get up in the morning and go to work in the factories that make the electronic instruments for your progressive pop groups. Or perhaps in the garment-trade sweat-shops turning out these awful pantomime clothes you insist on wearing. Or to fuel the jet-planes that take your friends to Katmandu.

YOUNG FRANK: Fine.

(*Comes down, stands near him.*)

FRANK: I'm making the point that your rejection of bourgeois society is a piece of cant until you reject the muck it produces.

YOUNG FRANK: I know you are.

FRANK: *I* reject it more than you do. *I* live more frugally than your lot.

YOUNG FRANK (*smiling*): My lot.

FRANK: I don't accept this society either. In fact, less than you do.

100

YOUNG FRANK: Fantastic.

FRANK (*snapping fingers in parody of youth*): Oh, great, man! All the way! Out of sight!

(YOUNG FRANK *shrugs and moves away again.*)

I've a far more defined view of the world I want than you and your lot. You heard my manifesto?

YOUNG FRANK: If I were——

FRANK: If I were King. Or President or whatever. First——

(*Lists on fingers, as* CHARLES *did.*)

ban all heavy transport using quiet residential streets to convey another load of sea-dredged aggregates. Then ban private cars entirely from city centres. Give the towns back to the pedestrians before we're all asphyxiated. Next: ban motor-bikes to anyone under forty and over fifty. Go for strictly limited aims, you see? Politics is the art of the possible. But step by step I'm closing down the motor industry, because how any government can encourage the production of more and more traffic is beyond my comprehension. You listening, man?

YOUNG FRANK (*looks at watch*): Yeah.

FRANK: So. Cars, lorries, motor-bikes. Discontinue the practice of filling our skies with supersonic aircraft to carry Yankee film producers and soft-drink salesmen around their empires. Legislate against luxury. I loathe luxury. We did very well without it during the war. Very well without cars and expense accounts and the grotesque inequality of the present day. The cult of youth.

(*Looks at his son for a reaction but he returns patiently, hands in pockets, to stand waiting for the end of his speech.*)

The cult of age. All that boutique nostalgia that tries to make out those lousy thirties and forties Hollywood films were nice and wholesome. Films so malevolent we took years painfully outgrowing our innocent acceptance of them. What else? Oh, yes. Worst of all—liberty. Everyone doing what they want. Free enterprise. Only means the bullies come out top. Only leads to traffic jams.

YOUNG FRANK: Dad.

FRANK: What?

YOUNG FRANK: I'm a bit short, as a matter of fact. I wondered if you could let me have a pound.

FRANK: Need the old man when it comes to bread. Eh?

YOUNG FRANK: Yeah.

FRANK: Doesn't your mother give you enough?

YOUNG FRANK: I don't like to ask her.

FRANK: She gets nearly all I earn.

YOUNG FRANK: You married her. You left her.

FRANK: Yes, well, that was an attempt to break up one of these bourgeois institutions. I left that off the list: the family. We will have no more marriages.

YOUNG FRANK: Very handy.

FRANK (*takes out wallet*): The family presupposes preference. Means people put their nearest and dearest first. Surely your new paradise won't allow that degree of discrimination. The family will have to go, Bill, along with nation, class, creed. Won't it?

YOUNG FRANK: Dunno.

FRANK: Time you did. How is she?

YOUNG FRANK: She's all right.

FRANK: And Jenny and Matthew?

YOUNG FRANK: Great, yeah.

(FRANK *gives him two notes.*)

FRANK: There's two.

YOUNG FRANK: Sure you can spare it?

FRANK: I live modestly.

YOUNG FRANK: Okay. Thanks. See you.

FRANK: Good-bye. Mind how you go on that bike. Ask Tom to keep it quiet.

(YOUNG FRANK *goes, slamming door.* FRANK *winces at noise.*)
Great coon! Oh, listen to me. Like some Andy Pandy twitched about by old Butterfingers up there.
(*Moves puppet-like across.*)
But if he let go, perhaps I'd fall to the floor. We're all in the genetic trap. However highly we regard ourselves, we owe our being to some unlikely people we meet at Christmas. We struggle at the end of our strings but here we are with our father's hands . . . our mother's sneeze . . . their middle-

aged indigestion. . . .

(*He takes out and lights a cigarette. Looks at the contents of his case.*)

But just imagine—you could be packing to go off *on your own* tomorrow. On a refresher course at some college— where? Yorkshire? Catching the train . . . the wartime feel of the station . . . we'll meet again and the Chattanooga Choo-Choo and I haven't said thanks for that lovely week-end. . . . Slightly smiling woman sharing my compartment . . . you going all the way? . . . All the way, she says, and suddenly without another word, she begins unbuttoning her coat. Her body——

(*Doorbell rings. Lights change.* FRANK *looks up, then goes off.* URSULA *comes on, present-day, aged 38. She is wearing an outdoor coat, gloves, etc., carrying a large bag with some materials, designs, etc. She leaves the door open.*)

URSULA: —can't think why I enjoy it so much. Even if the money wasn't so useful, I'd still go on taking these evening classes. I like schools when all the children have gone home.

(FRANK *follows her back and stands listening, nodding.*)

All the chairs up on their desks. I like the fact that these people of all ages and shapes and colours come along in their spare time to learn dress-making . . . have a chat . . . no one's pushing you to get you past exams . . . it's real teaching . . . how have you been? The kids slept soundly?

FRANK: Yes.

URSULA (*seeing suitcase open*): You have finished our packing?

FRANK: Um—well, I was just——

URSULA: I told you all that had to go in. Our sweaters, your jeans, your woollen socks to go inside your boots. And you put the four pairs of Wellies in the car?

FRANK: Ah—now——

URSULA: I stood here and told you every single thing that had to go in! I asked you if you wanted me to make a list but you said no, you could remember. What were you doing— dreaming again? Haven't you put the boots in then?

FRANK: Well, not yet. I was just——

URSULA: And what about the sick bags? The polythene bags in case Jenny's car-sick? She always is. D'you want it all over the safety-belts like last time?

FRANK: No.

URSULA: You haven't done that? I don't believe it. What about the ordnance survey maps from here to central Wales? You were going to look them out, d'you remember?

FRANK: They're in the—er——

URSULA: What *have* you done? Gone into another bloody dream? Oh, God, honestly! Have I got to do it again? And when? We're supposed to be getting off before dawn to miss the traffic and have as long in the country as possible! Now we shall have to do all this bloody packing in the dark and——

FRANK: No, I'll do it now.

URSULA: You won't. I'm dropping on my feet and if you potter about now you'll only wake me up again when you come blundering into bed. We'll do it in the morning. And even as I say that, I know I mean: *I'll* do it in the morning because nothing wakes you until the last possible moment.

FRANK: D'you know what this trip started as?

URSULA: What?

FRANK: A second honeymoon. Your parents were supposed to be having the children and you and I——

URSULA: Well, they couldn't, as it turned out, could they? So that was the end of—

(*Looks round uneasily, sensing something.*)

What's that smell? The casserole! Have you only just had it then? The oven switched itself off at nine, I told you that, I told you to take it out soon after that before it got dried up or cooled off. Was it all right?

FRANK: Christ . . . d'you know, love, it must have slipped my—I'll have it now . . .

URSULA: You mean you haven't eaten it? Haven't eaten at all?

FRANK: Would you believe it, I had some fish and chips from round the corner?

URSULA: It took me half an hour to prepare that casserole. I haven't stopped all day. I nearly fell asleep in class tonight

104

. . . oh . . .

(*Groans and shakes head. Thinks again.*)

Fish and chips? Did you go and buy them?

FRANK: Yes.

URSULA: Left the children alone in the house?

FRANK: It was only ten minutes.

URSULA: When are you going to think of someone but yourself? When are you going to consider something, but your own precious comfort? The answer's never, isn't it? You never have and you never will. So not only did I manage all the housework and all the preparations for going away but most of the packing too and bathed the children and got their meal and washed that up and made you a casserole and took my class and what were you doing all that time?

FRANK (*quietly*): I was trying to——

URSULA: Standing about doing nothing!

(*Grabs bag, goes off other door, slams it behind her.* FRANK *holds his head.*)

FRANK: Can I stand much more of this? Oh, yes. Much more.

(*Music:* You Stepped Out of a Dream. YOUNG URSE *comes on from another door. She is wearing school hat, blue raincoat, white socks and shoes but nothing else.* FRANK *turns to her. She stands downstage of him and unbuttons her raincoat, opens it so that he can see her body. He stands where he is, devouring her with his eyes. She moves slowly towards him and embraces him. He caresses her beneath the coat. Door opens and* URSULA *looks in again.*)

URSULA: Don't bother with that at this time of night. I want to get to sleep.

(*Goes out, slamming the door. With a last kiss,* YOUNG URSE *steps back, wraps her coat around her and goes off the way she came, making one final obscene gesture at the door.* FRANK *closes the case and goes after* URSULA, *turning out the lights.*)

THE END

After their bows, the actors sing Forget-me-not Lane *and go off severally by the doors.*

105